www.wadsworth.com

www.wadsworth.com is the World Wide Web site for
Thomson Wadsworth and is your direct source to
dozens of online resources.

At *www.wadsworth.com* you can find out about
supplements, demonstration software, and student
resources. You can also send email to many of our
authors and preview new publications and exciting
new technologies.

www.wadsworth.com
Changing the way the world learns®

Current Perspectives
Readings from InfoTrac® College Edition

Sigelman and Rider's Life-Span Human Development

Current Perspectives
Readings from InfoTrac® College Edition

Sigelman and Rider's Life-Span Human Development

FIFTH EDITION

GABRIELA MARTORELL
Portland State University

THOMSON
™
WADSWORTH

Australia • Canada • Mexico • Singapore • Spain
United Kingdom • United States

THOMSON

™

WADSWORTH

Current Perspectives: Readings from InfoTrac® College Edition:
Sigelman and Rider's Life-Span Human Development, Fifth Edition
Gabriela Martorell

Senior Acquisitions Editor: *Michele Sordi*
Assistant Editor: *Jennifer Wilkinson*
Editorial Assistant: *Jessica Kim*
Marketing Manager: *Chris Caldeira*
Marketing Assistant: *Nicole Morinon*
Advertising Project Manager: *Joy Westberg*
Project Manager, Editorial Production:
  Christy Krueger
Creative Director: *Robert Hugel*

Print Buyer: *Karen Hunt*
Production Service: *Rozi Harris, Interactive*
  Composition Corporation
Permissions Editor: *Audrey Pettengill*
Cover Designer: *Larry Didona*
Cover Image: *Photolibrary.com/Photonica*
Cover and Text Printer: *Thomson West*
Compositor: *Interactive Composition Corporation*

Printed in the United States of America
1 2 3 4 5 6 7 09 08 07 06 05

For more information about our products,
contact us at:
Thomson Learning Academic Resource Center
1-800-423-0563

For permission to use material from this text
or product, submit a request online at
http://www.thomsonrights.com.
Any additional questions about permissions
can be submitted by email to
thomsonrights@thomson.com.

Library of Congress Control Number:
2005921503

ISBN 0-495-00724-2

Thomson Higher Education
10 Davis Drive
Belmont, CA 94002-3098
USA

Asia (including India)
Thomson Learning
5 Shenton Way
#01-01 UIC Building
Singapore 068808

Australia/New Zealand
Thomson Learning Australia
102 Dodds Street
Southbank, Victoria 3006
Australia

Canada
Thomson Nelson
1120 Birchmount Road
Toronto, Ontario M1K 5G4
Canada

UK/Europe/Middle East/Africa
Thomson Learning
High Holborn House
50–51 Bedford Row
London WC1R 4LR
United Kingdom

Latin America
Thomson Learning
Seneca, 53
Colonia Polanco
11560 Mexico
D.F. Mexico

Spain (including Portugal)
Thomson Paraninfo
Calle Magallanes, 25
28015 Madrid, Spain

Contents

ALEWIJN OTT, MONIQUE M.B. BRETELER, FRANS VAN HARSKAMP, JULES J. CLAUS, TISCHA J.M. VAN DER CAMMEN, DIEDERICK E. GROBBEE, and ALBERT HOFMAN

1

Understanding Life-Span Human Development

Gender, Driver Aggression, and Driver Violence: An Applied Evaluation

Dwight A. Hennessy (1) and David L. Wiesenthal

D rivers completed a questionnaire assessing the likelihood of engaging in mild forms of driver aggression, the frequency of past driver violence, and a disposition toward driver stress. Both male and female drivers reported similar levels of mild driver aggression, supporting the notion that context is important in arousing female aggression. In contrast, driver violence was more frequent among male drivers, demonstrating the relevance of behavioral form within gender linked aggression research. Suggestions for the existence of a gender difference in driver violence, but not mild driver aggression are offered. Finally, driver stress susceptibility was linked to both mild driver aggression and driver violence.

Sex Roles: A Journal of Research, June 2001, p661(16).

"Gender, Driver Aggression, and Driver Violence: An Applied Evaluation" by Dwight A. Hennessy and David L. Wiesenthal. © 2001 Plenum Publishing Corporation.

INTRODUCTION

Driver aggression has been defined as any behavior intended to physically, emotionally, or psychologically harm another within the driving environment (Hauber, 1980; Hennessy & Wiesenthal, 1999). Because of its relationship with traffic violations (Novaco, 1991) and traffic collisions (Matthews, Dorn, & Glendon, 1991), driver aggression represents a potential danger, either directly or indirectly, to all roadway users. The American Automobile Association (Mizell, 1996) has estimated that incidents of roadway aggression in the United States increased by more than 50% between 1990 and 1996. Similarly, elevated levels of driver aggression have also been noted worldwide (Sleek, 1996; Taylor, 1997). For example, following an argument over a parking spot, a 52-year-old man in Toronto, Canada, pulled another man through his car window, spat on and punched him, then dragged him for nearly a quarter of a kilometer. The victim suffered serious injuries after being run over by the assailant following his release from the moving vehicle (Levy, 1999). Rollins (1997) reported that a female driver near Melbourne, Australia, was chased, tormented and physically assaulted for more than 20 min by an angry male driver whom she had nearly struck when swerving to avoid an illegally parked car. Similarly, near London, England, an amateur rally driver bumped and pushed a smaller vehicle on three separate occasions, forcing it off the road and killing its two occupants. The perpetrator reported that he was angered because the victim was driving too slowly, thus preventing him from passing (BBC News, 1998).

Driver Stress and Mild Aggression

Driving is a common event that has been found to elicit elevated levels of stress and arousal, particularly in highly frustrating conditions, such as obstructed or congested traffic (Hennessy & Wiesenthal, 1997, 1999; Hennessy, Wiesenthal, & Kohn, in press; Novaco, Stokols, & Milanesi, 1990; Rasmussen, Knapp, & Garner, 2000; Stokols & Novaco, 1981; Wiesenthal, Hennessy, & Totten, 2000b). In fact, a recent survey found that rush hour congestion was the most prevalent source of daily stress among U.K. drivers (BBC News, 2000). Subsequently, under conditions of stress, drivers are more likely to exhibit mild forms of driver aggression, including horn honking, swearing, and yelling at other drivers (Gulian, Matthews, Glendon, Davies, & Debney, 1989b; Hartley & El Hassani, 1994; Hennessy & Wiesenthal, 1997, 1999; Wiesenthal, Hennessy, & Gibson, 2000a). For many, the inability to deal effectively with stressful driving demands contributes to feelings of frustration, irritation, and anger, which can subsequently enhance the potential for driver aggression (Deffenbacher, Huff, Lynch, Oetting, & Salvatore, 2000; Ellison, Govern, Petri, & Figler, 1995; Joint, 1995; Matthews et al., 1998; Matthews, Tsuda, Xin, & Ozeki, 1999; Mizell, 1996).

It has recently been argued that the increased incidence of roadway aggression can be linked to a steady increase in traffic volume, congestion, and resulting driver stress over recent decades (Donelly, 1998; Hennessy, 2000; Taylor, 1997). The increase in the number of vehicles on the road has not been matched by a corresponding expansion of public roadways (Donelly, 1998). As a result of this greater competition for space, congestion levels, frustration, irritation, anger, and aggression have escalated. As traffic congestion increases, other drivers represent obstacles that impede the attainment of specific goals, such as driving at a certain speed or arriving at a destination in a specific time frame (Broome, 1985; Novaco, Stokols, Campbell, & Stokols, 1979). In this respect, aggression is often directed toward other drivers who are perceived to be the source of frustration and irritation (Gulian, Debney, Glendon, Davies, & Matthews, 1989a; Hennessy, 2000).

Mild Driver Aggression Versus Driver Violence

Naturalistic investigations of driver aggression have traditionally focused on horn honking as the primary manifestation of aggressive behavior. Generally, the frequency and duration of horn honking have been found to increase, and latency to decrease, among frustrated or irritated drivers (Anderson, 1989; Bradley, 1991; Doob & Gross, 1968; Ellison et al., 1995; Gulian et al., 1989b; Kenrick & MacFarlane, 1986; McDonald & Wooten, 1988; Wiesenthal et al., 2000a, 2000b). However, according to Novaco (1991), horn honking may actually represent the expression of anger or annoyance rather than true aggression. Novaco (1991) has proposed that driver aggression should be operationally defined by more severe and potentially destructive behaviors (e.g., roadside confrontations, chasing other drivers, throwing objects, or drive-by shootings), due to their greater potential for harm. Alternatively, Hennessy (2000) has noted that the extremely aggressive behaviors highlighted by Novaco (1991) could be more accurately described as driver violence, with less severe actions, such as horn honking, swearing and yelling, defined as mild driver aggression. Mild driver aggression is a fairly common response among frustrated drivers, whereas driver violence is a more atypical form of driving behavior representing a danger to all road users. Despite the fact that the immediate danger from mild aggression is minimal compared to driver violence, a single act of aggression has the potential to escalate to more frequent and life threatening actions (Hennessy, 1999).

Gender Differences in Aggressive Behavior

Males have generally been regarded as more likely to demonstrate aggressive behavior and to hold more favorable attitudes toward aggression (Harris & Knight-Bohnhoff, 1996; Lindeman, Harakka, & Keltikangas-Jarvinen, 1997; Tomada & Schneider, 1997). However, critics have argued against the general notion of the "nonaggressive" female (Fry & Gabriel, 1994; Pearson, 1997; White & Kowalski, 1994). Historically, research has narrowly focused on male behavior patterns, specifically overt or physical aggression, which has led to an underestimation of female aggression (Bjorkqvist, Osterman, & Kaukiainen,

1992; Fry & Gabriel, 1994). In fact, when alternate forms of expression are examined, female aggression is much more prevalent than previously reported (Bjorkqvist et al., 1992). Specifically, indirect aggression, in which other individuals or social structures are used to harm a target, is more common among females compared to males, whereas there is little evidence of gender differences in the use of verbal aggression (Bettencourt & Miller, 1996; Bjorkqvist & Niemela, 1992; Eron, 1992; Lagerspetz, Bjorkqvist, & Peltonen, 1988). By broadening the conceptualization of "aggression" beyond physical behaviors, a more accurate depiction of female aggression has begun to emerge.

Bettencourt and Miller (1996) have also argued that an overreliance on laboratory research has contributed to a distorted perception of female aggression. The prevalence of male aggression in Western cultures is largely because of traditional gender role socialization, which encourages highly assertive, dangerous and risky behaviors among men, including aggression and violence (Eagley & Steffen, 1986; Greenglass & Noguchi, 1996). In contrast, females are typically socialized to display passivity and tolerance under frustrating or irritating conditions and to refrain from aggressive behavior (Eron, 1992; Greenglass & Noguchi, 1996; White & Kowalski, 1994). Thus, in laboratory studies of aggression, social desirability may serve to repress aggressive behavior among females, while prompting it among males. As a result, Bjorkqvist et al. (1992) has advocated the greater use of naturalistic investigations and contextual information in research to more accurately understand female aggression.

Mild Aggression Among Female Drivers

The driving environment is one naturalistic context in which evidence of female aggression has escalated (Joint, 1995; Novaco, 1991). Using a self report "road rage" index, the Australian Associated Motor Insurers (1997) reported that female drivers were as likely to demonstrate extreme forms of driver aggression as males. Similarly, in an American sample, Hauber (1980) also found male and female drivers were equally likely to target mild forms of aggression, such as horn honking and fist shaking, toward a confederate pedestrian attempting to cross at an intersection. Further Hennessy and Wiesenthal (1997, 1999) have interviewed participants while they were commuting in highway traffic conditions to examine the influence of various personal and situational factors on mild driver aggression. They have consistently found that female drivers are equally likely as male drivers to exhibit mild aggressive behaviors toward other drivers, including horn honking, swearing, yelling, and purposely tailgating, regardless of traffic congestion level and despite a greater tendency for males to demonstrate a vengeful attitude (Hennessy & Wiesenthal, 1997, 1999; Wiesenthal & Hennessy, 1999; Wiesenthal et al., 2000a). One likely explanation for the prevalence of aggression among females in this context is that the driving environment provides an element of anonymity for all drivers (Hennessy, 1999; Lightdale & Prentice, 1994; Mann, Newton, & Innes, 1982; Wiesenthal & Janovjak, 1992). Previous research has established that general aggressive tendencies increase with perceptions of anonymity and deindividuation (Rehm, Steinleitner, & Lilli, 1987; Rogers & Ketchen, 1979; Yamaguchi, 1980), mainly because of the fact that anonymity reduces the risk of detection and reprimand for aggressive behavior (Freedman, 1982; Zimbardo, 1970). In this respect, protection from being identified as a female driver may reduce restraints against behaving aggressively toward other drivers (Lightdale & Prentice, 1994; Mann et al., 1982). Considering that gender role socialization has established greater restraints against aggressive behavior among females (Eagley & Steffen, 1986; Greenglass & Noguchi, 1996), the anonymity of the driving environment may simply provide a unique opportunity for females to breach traditional gender roles and express aggressive tendencies. In such situations, the fact that the automobile is a convenient means of escape and represents a legitimate weapon (Marsh & Collett, 1987), empowers female drivers and provides an opportunity to aggress, equal to that of males.

Hypotheses

1. There will be no gender differences in ratings of mild aggressive behaviors.
2. High stress drivers will report greater mild driver aggression than low stress drivers.
3. Males will demonstrate greater frequency of past violent driving behavior than females.
4. Driver violence will be greater among high stress drivers than low stress drivers.

METHOD

Participants

The present study included 122 female and 70 male participants from the student and employee populations of York University, as well as from the general Metropolitan Toronto population. Fifty-one participants were recruited from the undergraduate research participant pool at York University and received one experimental credit for their involvement (n = 34 females and n = 17 males). All others were obtained as voluntary participants through posted signs, personal contact, and word of mouth.

All participants commuted on a daily basis and a minimum of 3 years driving experience was required. The average was 8.75 years experience (M = 7.02 years for female and M = 11.77 years for male drivers) and their ages ranged from 19 to 68 years, with an average of 26.22 years (M = 25.83 years for female and M = 28.60 years for male drivers). The average driving time ranged from 15 to 270 min per day, with an average of 93.96 min per day (M = 94.19 min for female and M = 93.57 min for male drivers).

Measures

Driving Behaviour Inventory—General (DBI-Gen)

Driver stress was measured using the Driving Behaviour Inventory-General Driver Stress scale (DBI-Gen; Gulian et al., 1989b). The DBI-Gen consists of 16 items that tap a general disposition, or "trait" susceptibility, to driver stress. Previous research has established the DBI-Gen as a valid and reliable measure of trait driver stress across cultures (Glendon et al., 1993; Hennessy & Wiesenthal, 1999; Lajunen, Corry, Summala, & Hartley, 1998; Matthews et al., 1991, 1999). Hennessy and Wiesenthal (1997) have found the DBI-Gen to accurately predict actual stress levels measured in both low and high traffic congestion. In the present study, responses were made on a Likert scale ranging from 0 to 100, indicating the level of agreement with each statement, rather than on the original 0 to 4 Likert scale. Previous research has shown this revision to maintain high reliability (alpha = .90; Hennessy & Wiesenthal, 1997). Scoring consisted of the mean response to the 16 items, with higher scores indicating greater trait driver stress susceptibility.

Self Report Driver Aggression

The Self Report Driver Aggression questionnaire was designed to tap general self report driving behavior patterns (Hennessy & Wiesenthal, 1999, in press). Items were based on behaviors identified by Gulian et al. (1989a) as common coping responses to driving demands, whereas other items were generated from interviews with highway commuters (Hennessy, 2000). Participants were asked to rate the likelihood of generally engaging in five mild aggressive be-haviors (i.e., horn honking out of frustration, swearing/yelling, purposeful tailgating, flashing high beams, and hand gestures). Responses were placed on a Likert scale ranging from 0 (not at all) to 5 (nearly all the time). An aggre-gate driver aggression score was calculated as the mean response to the five items. Hennessy (2000) has found that self reported driver aggression scores correlated highly with actual acts of aggression occurring in high congestion conditions (r = .643).

The Self Report Driver Violence questionnaire was designed in order to evaluate the frequency of personally initiated violent driving behaviors. Six items were introduced by Novaco (1991), whereas one item was identified through interviews with commuters (Hennessy, 2000). Participants were asked to indicate the frequency of previously initiating each of the violent driving behaviors (i.e., verbal confrontations, physical confrontations, chasing other vehicles, drive-by shootings, throwing objects, purposeful contact, and vandalizing vehicles). An aggregate violence score was calculated as the cumu-lative frequency of the individual violence items.

Procedure

Participants completed the DBI-Gen, the Self Report Driver Aggression ques-tionnaire, and the Self Report Driver Violence questionnaire anonymously.

Because of the sensitive nature of the present driving measures, instructions stressed the confidentiality of all responses.

RESULTS

Intercorrelations, means, standard deviations, and alpha reliabilities for the DBI–Gen, Self Report Driver Aggression, and Self Report Driver Violence questionnaires appear in Table 1. The DBI–Gen demonstrated the greatest internal consistency (alpha = .83), whereas the Self Report Driver Aggression and Self Report Driver Violence questionnaires demonstrated moderate reliability (alphas = .75 and .69 respectively).

Separate hierarchical entry stepwise regressions were used to determine predictors of mild driver aggression and driver violence. The procedure for each was to enter gender, age, and driver stress forcibly and add all cross product interactions stepwise on the first run. If any interactions were significant, they would be entered forcibly on the second run along with the implicated main effects. All other significant main effects would be added stepwise on the second run. However, in the event that no interactions proved significant on the first run, the main effects would be entered stepwise on the second run. This strategy has been reported elsewhere (e.g., Hennessy & Wiesenthal, in press; Kohn, Gurevich, Pickering, & Macdonald, 1994; Kohn & Macdonald, 1992). Table 2 contains the final regression models for mild driver aggression and driver violence.

Mild Driver Aggression

A mild driver aggression score was calculated as the mean response to individual aggression items. Higher scores represented a greater likelihood of

Table 1. Intercorrelations, Means, Standard Deviations, and Alpha Reliabilities for the Driving Behavior Inventory (DBI-Gen), Self Report Driver Aggression, Self Report Driver Violence, Age and Gender

	1	2	3	4	5
1. Driving Behavior Inventory-Gen	—	—	—	—	—
2. Self Report Driver Aggression	.57 (**)	—	—	—	—
3. Self Report Driver Violence	.27	.39 (**)	—	—	—
4. Driver age	−.40 (**)	−.24	−.12	—	—
5. Driver gender	−.00	.09	.23	.17	—
Mean	37.22	1.43	1.84	26.22	—
SD	17.23	0.85	4.50	10.39	—
Minimum	.63	0	0	19	—
Maximum	83.13	4.40	41.0	68	—
Cronbach alpha	.83	.75	.69	—	—

Note: n = 192.
(**)$p < .01$.

Table 2. Significant Predictors of Mild Driver Aggression and Driver Violence

Criterion	Predictor	b	t
Mild aggression (a)	Driver stress	0.281	9.66 (**)
	Intercept	0.381	3.19
Driver violence (b)	Driver stress	2.193	3.45 (**)
	Driver gender	0.710	4.00 (**)
	Intercept	−3.786	−3.34

Note. n = 192.
(a)R^2 = 0.33, $F_{(1,191)}$ = 93.65, $p < .01$.
(b)R^2 = 0.13, $F_{(2,189)}$ = 13.93, $p < .01$
(**)$p < .01$.

exhibiting mild driver aggression. Mild aggression was predicted by the main effect of driver stress (see Table 2). Hypothesis 1 was confirmed in that the likelihood of exhibiting mild aggression was similar for male and female drivers. Also, consistent with hypothesis 2, mild driver aggression increased with a driver stress susceptibility, where high trait stress drivers reported greater mild driver aggression than low stress drivers.

Driver Violence

An aggregate driver violence score was calculated as the total frequency of the individual violence items. Higher scores represented a greater frequency of initiating past violent driving behaviors. Driver violence was predicted by the main effects of driver gender and driver stress (see Table 2). Consistent with hypothesis 3, male drivers reported greater frequency of past violent driving behaviors than female drivers. Hypothesis 4 was also confirmed in that high stress drivers reported greater violence than low stress drivers.

It should be noted that because of the low base rate of driver violence, the distribution of violence scores was positively skewed. Despite this fact, the present study demonstrated a link between violence, stress, and gender at the higher limits of violence scores, where relationships are underestimated by multiple regression analysis, and no link at the lower limits of violence scores, where relationships are overestimated (see Tabachnik & Fidell, 1989).

Comparing Individual Driving Behaviors

To evaluate potential gender differences in the likelihood of individual driving behaviors, a MANOVA was performed with driver gender as the independent variable and individual mild aggressive and violent driving behaviors as the dependent variables. In terms of mild aggressive behaviors, males demonstrated a greater likelihood of flashing high beams at other drivers compared to females (M = 1.57 vs. M = 0.97, see Table 3). Driver gender did not differentiate any other individual mild aggressive behavior.

Table 3. Comparison of the Mean Likelihood of Individual Mild Aggressive Behaviors

	Males	Females	F(1, 190)
Horn honking	2.13 (1.15)	2.21 (1.23)	0.21
Swearing/yelling	1.63 (1.25)	1.71 (1.51)	0.15
Flashing high beams	1.57 (1.33)	0.97 (1.16)	10.90 (**)
Purposeful tailgating	1.33 (1.10)	1.04 (1.11)	3.00
Hand gestures	1.04 (0.86)	0.92 (1.04)	0.72

Note. SD are bracketed.
$(**)p < .01$.

Table 4. Comparison of the Frequency of Past Acts of Individual Violent Driving Behaviors

	Males	Females	F(1,190)
Chasing	1.19 (2.11)	0.54 (1.34)	6.71 (**)
Verbal confrontations	1.03 (2.71)	0.19 (0.66)	10.63 (**)
Vandalizing vehicles	0.51 (1.73)	0.15 (0.62)	4.46 (*)
Physical confrontations	0.29 (1.25)	0.02 (0.18)	5.46 (*)
Throwing objects	0.20 (0.77)	0.07 (0.28)	3.01
Purposeful contact	0.02 (0.12)	0.06 (0.29)	1.35
Drive-by shootings	0.01 (0.12)	0.04 (0.45)	0.23

Note. SD are bracketed.
$(*)p < .05$.
$(**)p < .01$.

For both males and females, past acts of driver violence were infrequent, although chasing other drivers and verbal confrontations were the most frequent violent actions (see Table 4). Males were more likely than females to report past incidents of chasing other drivers, verbal roadside confrontations, vandalizing other vehicles, and physical roadside confrontations.

DISCUSSION

Driver Gender, Aggression, and Violence

As anticipated, and consistent with previous research (Hennessy & Wiesenthal, 1997, 1999), the present study failed to demonstrate a general gender difference in the likelihood of mild driver aggression. Female drivers reported equivalent tendencies toward mild aggression as male drivers. Despite the prevailing notion that men are generally more aggressive than females, the present study highlights the importance of contextual information in evaluating the prevalence of female aggression (see Bjorkqvist et al., 1992; Deaux & Major,

1987; Eagley, 1987). The driving environment represents a unique setting that is equally conducive to aggression among male and female drivers. Considering that the vehicle itself represents a very powerful and dangerous weapon possessed by all drivers (Marsh & Collett, 1987), the ability to aggress is equalized across gender. In situations where drivers perceive that they have been placed at risk or wronged in some way by another driver, fear, anger, and perceptions of provocation may result (Wiesenthal et al., 2000a), which have previously been found to heighten the potential for female aggression (Bettencourt & Miller, 1996; Blanchard & Blanchard, 1992; Fraczek, 1992; Frodi, Macaulay, & Thorne, 1977).

Anonymity and deindividuation within the driving environment may also contribute to the escalation of female aggression. Because of the low probability of repeated interactions or contact with other drivers, it is often difficult to specifically identify an individual driver as male or female. As a result, anonymous drivers are more prone to defy restraints against harming others (Novaco, 1991). Considering that females have traditionally been socialized to refrain from aggressive behavior (Eagley & Steffen, 1986), the anonymity of the driving environment and perceptions of deindividuation represent a unique opportunity for liberation from gender roles, thus facilitating the expression of aggressive tendencies. Further, the potential for personal repercussions as a result of aggressive behaviors are minimized with anonymity, leading to a heightened sense of control over victims. This inability to identify a driver as female may contribute to feelings of power and control over other drivers, increasing the potential for anti-normative behaviors (i.e., mild aggression) among female drivers (Lightdale & Prentice, 1994).

The present findings have also demonstrated the importance of the form of aggressive behavior in evaluating gender differences. Specifically, violent driving behavior was more pronounced among males compared to females. According to Meerloo (1968), violence can be defined as a more extreme manifestation of aggressive behavior. Similarly, Hennessy (1999) has classified driver violence as a distinct category of driving behaviors that are more severe and potentially dangerous than milder aggression.

One possible explanation for this gender difference may be that violent driving behaviors involve a predominance of overt or physical actions directed toward other drivers. According to Buss and Perry (1992), males are more prone to exhibit physical or overt aggression than females. Violent driving behaviors also require prolonged contact with a victim, which likely minimizes perceptions of anonymity and heightens the potential for reprimand or reciprocal acts of aggression and violence. In the present study, males demonstrated a greater tendency toward physical confrontations, verbal confrontations, chasing other drivers, and automobile vandalism compared to females, which are more likely to involve physical proximity to a victim than are mild aggressive behaviors.

Another potential reason for the gender difference in driver violence may be that female drivers are more restrained in situations representing personal risk or danger. According to Berkowitz (1988), the fear that aggressive behavior could lead to retaliation may reduce aggressive tendencies. Compared to males, females are generally more accurate at predicting the potential for harm and future repercussions within dangerous or risky situations (Eagley & Steffen, 1986). Within the driving environment, this tendency may lead females to avoid violent actions due to the elevated risk of personal injury. Considering that violent actions represent greater potential for harm than mild aggressive behaviors, female drivers may endure mild aggression fearing its escalation to violence compared to male drivers.

The Impact of Stress on Aggression and Violence

Previous research has found that psychological stress can heighten the potential for general aggressive behavior (Cohen, 1980; Hennessy & Wiesenthal, 1997; Wiesenthal et al., 2000a). The present study found that both males and females who perceived the driving environment as stressful reported a greater likelihood of engaging in mild forms of driver aggression. Driver stress has been described as a consequence of negative evaluations of driving stimuli, leading to irritation, frustration, and negative affect (Gulian et al., 1989b; Hartley & El Hassani, 1994; Hennessy & Wiesenthal, 1997). Under such conditions, highly stressed drivers are more likely to perceive other drivers as the source of frustration (Gulian et al., 1989a; Hennessy, 2000) and to interpret undesirable actions from other drivers as personal and purposeful behaviors, leading to increased aggression (Wiesenthal et al., 2000a).

High stress drivers were also found to report elevated incidents of past driving violence compared to low stress drivers. Despite the fact that driver violence has been considered in the present study as a more extreme and potentially dangerous form of driver aggression, little research has been conducted regarding the antecedents of violence compared to aggression. It is possible that among a small segment of drivers, the irritation and frustration experienced in stressful conditions contribute to violent behavior. However, previous evidence of this process is unclear. It is also probable that consideration of other personal and situational factors is necessary to more fully understand the link between stress and violence. For example, driving vengeance, which is the desire to harm other drivers in response to a perceived injustice, is more common among male drivers and among those under the influence of driver stress (Hennessy, 2000; Wiesenthal et al., 2000a). Considering that violent drivers in the present study were predominantly male, it is possible that a vengeful attitude contributed to the association between stress and violence. Further research is needed to more clearly understand the antecedents and consequences of driver violence.

Limitations of the Present Study

One limitation of the present study was the fact that self report measures of behavior and stress were used, which lack contextual information present in actual driving situations. According to Hennessy (2000), aggressive behavior does not occur in isolation, but is partially determined by aspects within the instigating environment, such as traffic congestion and provocation from other drivers. In a similar respect, driver stress has also been found to be highly dependent on the interaction of situational and individual factors (Hennessy & Wiesenthal, 1997). As a result, responses in the present study may not have accurately reflected true behavioral tendencies or stress reactions that occur in actual traffic situations. Another problem was that the female sample was slightly younger and less experienced than the male sample. Previous research has found that age is negatively related to both driver stress and aggression (Gibson & Wiesenthal, 1996; Hauber, 1980). Although small, the age difference may account for elevated aggression among the female sample. Future research should employ a more diverse age sample in order to present a clearer analysis of driver stress, aggression, and violence. Finally, the chosen behavior measures used a forced choice response method. It is possible that the limited options provided were those that masked potential gender differences in aggression, while highlighting gender differences in driver violence. The use of open-ended behavior responses in future research could provide a wider variety of possible behavior outcomes.

ACKNOWLEDGMENTS

This manuscript is based on research conducted by Dwight Hennessy in partial fulfilment of the Ph.D. degree requirements of York University. The research was supervised by Professor David Wiesenthal. The authors wish to thank Professors Esther Greenglass and James Check, who served on Dwight Hennessy's dissertation committee, as well as Dr. Bob Lamble of the Ontario Ministry of Transportation for their assistance. Further, valuable assistance was provided by Alex Shanahan, Suzan Krepostman, Amy Harris, and Mike Foundos. This research was partially supported by a grant from the Ontario Ministry of Transportation. Opinions expressed in this report are those of the authors and do not necessarily reflect the views and policies of the Ministry.

(1) To whom correspondence should be addressed at Department of Psychology, State University of New York College at Buffalo, 1300 Elmwood Avenue, Buffalo, New York 14222.

CRITICAL THINKING QUESTIONS

1. The authors make the claim that one of the reasons that male aggression is more prevalent than female aggression in Western societies is due to traditional gender role socialization. Specifically, they claim that Western cultures encourage "highly assertive, dangerous, and risky behaviors among men," while women are socialized to display "passivity and tolerance

under frustrating or irritating conditions and to refrain from aggressive behaviors." In the current study, gender differences were found for men and women in comparing their likelihood of engaging in driver violence, but no gender differences were found for mild driver aggression. Why would socialization of traditional gender roles make a difference in one context, but not the other?

2. The authors state that psychological stress can heighten the potential for aggressive behaviors. Furthermore, the results of this study suggest that males are more likely to engage in violent confrontations with other drivers. Although this gender difference for driver violence is explained as a function of different socialization practices for men and women, speculate on how potential differences in resiliency in the face of stress might impact driver violence.

3. In this study, driver violence was defined with six items (i.e., verbal confrontations, physical confrontations, chasing other vehicles, drive-by shootings, throwing objects, purposeful contact, and vandalizing vehicles). These events were relatively rare for both genders, and especially so for females. How might the relative scarcity of these behaviors affect the data? In what ways might this bias your conclusions?

REFERENCES

Anderson, C. A. (1989). Temperature and aggression: Ubiquitous effects of heat on the occurrence of human violence. *Psychological Bulletin, 106,* 74–96.

Australian Associated Motor Insurers. (1997, September 17). Media Release. AAMI Insurance Association.

BBC News. (1998, March 30). Double death driver in court. BBC News Online [On-line]. Available: http://haddock.org/matt/bbcnews.html

BBC News. (2000, November 1). Commuting is "biggest stress." BBC News Online [On-line]. Available: http://news.bbc.co. uklhilenglishlhealthlnewsid.999000/999961.stm

Berkowitz, L. (1988). Frustrations, appraisals, and aversively stimulated aggression. *Aggressive Behavior, 10,* 59–73.

Bettencourt, B. A., & Miller, N. (1996). Gender differences in aggression as a function of provocation: A meta-analysis. *Psychological Bulletin, 119,* 422–447.

Bjorkqvist, K., & Niemela, P. (1992). New trends in the study of female aggression. In K. Bjorkqvist & P. Niemela (Eds.), *Of mice and women: Aspects of female aggression* (pp. 3–16). New York: Academic Press.

Bjorkqvist, K., Osterman, K., & Kaukiainen, A. (1992). The development of direct and indirect aggressive strategies in males and females. In

K. Bjorkqvist & P. Niemela (Eds.), *Of mice and women: Aspects of female aggression* (pp. 51–64). New York: Academic Press.

Blanchard, D. C., & Blanchard, R. J. (1992). Sex, drugs, and defensive behavior: Implications for animal models of defense. In K. Bjorkqvist & P. Niemela (Eds.), *Of mice and women: Aspects of female aggression* (pp. 318–329). New York: Academic Press.

Bradley, D. R. (1991). Anatomy of a DATASIM simulation: The Doob and Gross horn honking study. *Behavior Research Methods, Instruments, and Computers, 23,* 190–207.

Broome, M. R. (1985). The implication of driver stress. Proceedings of the Planning and Transportation Research and Computation (PTRC) Seminar N., Summer Meeting (Vol. P270). London, UK: PTRC Education Research Services Ltd.

Buss, A. H., & Perry, M. (1992). The Aggression Questionnaire. *Journal of Personality and Social Psychology, 63,* 452–459.

Cohen, S. (1980). Aftereffects of stress on human performance and social behavior: A review of research and theory. *Psychological Bulletin, 88,* 82–108.

Deaux, K. K., & Major, B. (1987). Putting gender into context: An interactive model of gender related behavior. *Psychological Review, 94,* 369–389.

Deffenbacher, J. L., Huff, M. E., Lynch, R. S., Getting, E. R., & Salvatore, N. F. (2000). Characteristics and treatment of high-anger drivers. *Journal of Consulting Psychology, 47,* 5–17.

Donelly, S. B. (1998, January 12). Road rage. *Time,* 44–48.

Doob, A. N., & Gross, A. E. (1968). Status of frustrator as an inhibitor of horn honking responses. *Journal of Social Psychology, 76,* 213–218.

Eagley, A. H. (1987). *Gender differences in social behavior: A social-role interpretation.* Hillsdale, NJ: Erlbaum.

Eagley, A. H., & Steffen, V. J. (1986). Gender and aggressive behavior: A meta-analytic review of the social psychological literature. *Psychological Bulletin, 100,* 309–330.

Ellison, P. A., Govern, J. M., Petri, H. L., & Figler, M. H. (1995). Anonymity and aggressive driving behavior: A field study. *Journal of Social Behavior and Personality, 10,* 265–272.

Eron, L. D. (1992). Gender differences in violence: Biology and/or socialization? In K. Bjorkqvist & P. Niemela (Eds.), *Of mice and women: Aspects of female aggression* (pp. 89–97). New York: Academic Press.

Fraczek, A. (1992). Patterns of aggressive-hostile behavior orientation among adolescent boys and girls. In K. Bjorkqvist & P. Niemela (Eds.), *Of mice and women: Aspects of female aggression* (pp. 107–112). New York: Academic Press.

Freedman, J. L. (1982). Theories of contagion as they relate to mass psychogenic illness. In M. J. Colligan, J. W Pennebaker, & L. R. Murphy (Eds.), *Mass psychogenic illness* (pp. 171–182). Hillsdale, NJ: Erlbaum.

Frodi, A., Macaulay, J., & Thome, P. R. (1977). Are women always less aggressive than men? A review of the experimental literature. *Psychological Bulletin, 84,* 634–660.

Fry, D. P., & Gabriel, A. H. (1994). The cultural construction of gender and aggression. *Sex Roles, 30,* 165–167.

Gibson, P. M., & Wiesenthal, D. L. (1996). The Driving Vengeance Questionnaire: The development of a scale to measure deviant drivers' attitudes. LaMarsh Research Programme Report Series: Vol. 54. LaMarsh Research Programme on Violence and Conflict Resolution. Toronto, Canada: York University.

Glendon, A. I., Dorn, L., Matthews, G., Gulian, E., Davies, D. R., & Debney, L. M. (1993). Reliability of the Driving Behaviour Inventory. *Ergonomics, 36,* 719–726.

Greenglass, E. R., & Noguchi, K. (1996). Longevity, gender, and health: A psychocultural perspective. Position paper presented at the first meeting of the International Society of Health Psychology, Montreal, Canada.

Gulian, E., Debney, L. M., Glendon, A. I., Davies, D. R., & Matthews, G. (1989a). Coping with driver stress. In F. McGuigan, W. E. Sime, & J. M. Wallace (Eds.), *Stress and tension control* (Vol. 3, pp. 173–186). New York: Plenum Press.

Gulian, E., Matthews, G., Glendon, A. I., Davies, D. R., & Debney, L. M. (1989b). Dimensions of driver stress. *Ergonomics, 32,* 585–602.

Harris, M. B., & Knight–Bohnhoff, K. (1996). Gender and aggression: II. Personal aggressiveness. *Sex Roles, 35,* 27–42.

Hartley, L. R., & El Hassani, J. (1994). Stress, violations, and accidents. *Applied Ergonomics, 25,* 221–230.

Hauber, A. R. (1980). The social psychology of driving behavior and the traffic environment: Research on aggressive behavior in traffic. *International Review of Applied Psychology, 29,* 461–474.

Hennessy, D. A. (1999). Evaluating driver aggression. Unpublished Major Area Paper. Toronto, Canada: York University.

Hennessy, D. A. (2000). The interaction of person and situation within the driving environment: Daily hassles, traffic congestion, driver stress, aggression, vengeance and past performance. Dissertation Abstracts International: Section B: The Sciences and Engineering, 60, 8B, 4301.

Hennessy, D. A., & Wiesenthal, D. L. (1997). The relationship between traffic congestion, driver stress, and direct versus indirect coping behaviors. *Ergonomics, 40,* 348–361.

Hennessy, D. A., & Wiesenthal, D. L. (1999). Traffic congestion, driver stress, and driver aggression. *Aggressive Behavior, 25,* 409–423.

Hennessy, D. A., & Wiesenthal, D. L. (in press). Further validation of the Driving Vengeance Questionnaire (DVQ). Violence and Victims.

Hennessy, D. A., Wiesenthal, D. L., & Kohn, P. M. (in press). The influence of traffic congestion, daily hassles, and trait stress susceptibility on state driver stress: An interactive perspective. *Journal of Applied Biobehavioral Research, 5,* 162–179.

Joint, M. (1995). Road rage. Report prepared for the American Automobile Association: Group public policy road safety unit. Washington, DC: AAA Foundation for Traffic Safety.

Kenrick, D., & MacFarlane, S. (1986). Ambient temperature and horn honking: A field study of the heat/aggression relationship. *Environment and Behavior, 18,* 179–191.

Kohn, P. M., Gurevich, M., Pickering, D. I., & Macdonald, J. E. (1994). Alexithymia, reactivity, and the adverse impact of hassles based stress. *Personality and Individual Differences, 16,* 805–812.

Kohn, P. M., & Macdonald, J. E. (1992). Hassles, anxiety, and negative well-being. *Anxiety Stress, and Coping, 5,* 151–163.

Lagerspetz, K., Bjorkqvist, K., & Peltonen, T. (1988). Is indirect aggression typical of females? Gender differences in aggressiveness in 11 to 12 year old children. *Aggressive Behavior, 14,* 403–404.

Lajunen, T., Corry, A., Summala, H., & Hartley, L. (1998). Cross cultural differences in driver self assessments of their perceptual motor and safety skills: Australian and Finns. *Personality and Individual Differences, 24,* 539–550.

Levy, L. (1999, May 4). Road rage driver jailed. *Toronto Star.*

Lightdale, J. R., & Prentice, T. A. (1994). Rethinking sex differences in aggression: Aggressive behavior in the absence of social roles. *Personality and Social Psychology Bulletin, 20,* 34–44.

Lindeman, M., Harakka, T., & Keltikangas-Jarvinen, L. (1997). Age and gender differences in adolescent reactions to conflict situations: Aggression, prosociality, and withdrawal. *Journal of Youth and Adolescence, 26,* 339–351.

Mann, L., Newton, J. W., & Tones, J. M. (1982). A test between deindividuation and emergent norm theories of crowd aggression. *Journal of Personality and Social Psychology, 42,* 260–272.

Marsh, P., & Collett, P. (1987). The car as a weapon. *Et Cetera, 44,* 146–151.

Matthews, G., Dorn, L., & Glendon, A. I. (1991). Personality correlates of driver stress. *Personality and Individual Differences, 12,* 535–549.

Matthews, G., Dorn, L., Hoyes, T. W., Davies, D. R., Glendon, A. I., & Taylor, R. G. (1998). Driver stress and performance on a driving simulator. *Human Factors, 40,* 136–149.

Matthews, G., Tsuda, A., Xin, C., & Ozeki, Y. (1999). Individual differences in driver stress vulnerability in a Japanese sample. *Ergonomics, 42,* 401–415.

McDonald, P. J., & Wooten, S. A. (1988). The influence of incompatible responses on the reduction of aggression: An alternate explanation. *Journal of Social Psychology, 128,* 401–406.

Meerloo, J. A. M. (1968). Human violence versus animal aggression. *Psychoanalytic Review, 55,* 37–56.

Mizell, L. (1996). Aggressive driving. Research report for the American Automobile Association: Foundation for traffic safety. Washington, DC: AAA Foundation for Traffic Safety.

Novaco, R. W. (1991). Aggression on roadways. In R. Baenninger (Ed.), *Targets of violence and aggression* (pp. 253–326). North-Holland: Elsevier Science Publisher.

Novaco, R. W., Stokols, D., Campbell, J., & Stokols, J. (1979). Transportation, stress, and community psychology. *American Journal of Community Psychology, 7,* 361–380.

Novaco, R. W., Stokols, D., & Milanesi, L. (1990). Objective and subjective dimensions of travel impedance as determinants of commuting stress. *American Journal of Community Psychology, 18,* 231–257.

Pearson, P. (1997). *When she was bad: Violent women and the myth of innocence.* Toronto: Random House.

Rasmussen, C., Knapp, T. J., & Garner, L. (2000). Driving induced stress in urban college students. *Perceptual and Motor Skills, 90,* 437–443.

Rehm, J., Steinleitner, M., & Lilli, W. (1987). Wearing uniforms and aggression: A field study. *European Journal of Social Psychology, 17,* 357–360.

Rogers, R. W., & Ketchen, C. M. (1979). Effects of anonymity an arousal on aggression. *Journal of Psychology, 102,* 13–19.

Rollins, A. (1997, October 23). It's all the rage. *The Age.*

Sleek, S. (1996). Car wars: Taming drivers' aggression. *APA Monitor, 27*(1), 13–14.

Stokols, D., & Novaco, R. W. (1981). Transportation and wellbeing. In G. Altman, J. F. Wohlwill, & P. B. Everett (Eds.), *Human behavior and environment (Vol. 5): Transportation and behavior.* London: Plenum Press.

Tabachnik, B. G., & Fidell, L. S. (1989). *Using multivariate statistics* (2nd ed.). New York: Harper & Row.

Taylor, B. (1997, August 25). Life in the slow lane. *Toronto Star,* D1.

Tomada, G., & Schneider, B. H. (1997). Relational aggression, gender, and peer acceptance: Invariance across culture, stability over time, and concordance among informants. *Developmental Psychology, 33,* 601–609.

White, J., & Kowalski, R. M. (1994). Deconstructing the myth of the nonaggressive woman: A feminist analysis. *Psychology of Women Quarterly, 18,* 487–508.

Wiesenthal, D. L., & Hennessy, D. A. (1999). Driver stress, vengeance, and aggression: What is "road rage." Proceedings of the Canadian Multidisciplinary Road Safety Conference XI, Halifax, Nova Scotia, Canada.

Wiesenthal, D. L., Hennessy, D. A., & Gibson, P. (2000a). The Driving Vengeance Questionnaire (DVQ): The development of a scale to measure deviant drivers' attitudes. *Violence and Victims, 15,* 115–136.

Wiesenthal, D. L., Hennessy, D. A., & Totten, B. (2000b). The influence of music on driver stress. *Journal of Applied Social Psychology, 30,* 1709–1719.

Wiesenthal, D. L., & Janovjak, D. P. (1992). Deindividuation and automobile driving behaviour. LaMarsh Research Programme Report Series: Vol 46. LaMarsh Research Programme on Violence and Conflict Resolution. Toronto, Canada: York University.

Yamaguchi, S. (1980). The effects of fear-arousal and anonymity upon aggressive behavior. *Japanese Journal of Experimental Social Psychology, 20,* 1–8.

Zimbardo, P. G. (1970). The human choice: Individuation, reason, and order versus deindividuation, impulse, and chaos. In W. J. Arnold & D. Levine (Eds.), *Nebraska symposium on motivation (Vol. 17).* Lincoln: University of Nebraska Press.

2

Theories of Human Development

A Pregnant Mother's Diet May Turn the Genes Around

Sandra Blakeslee

New research on epigenetics or change in gene function by environmental factors with no DNA-sequence alteration.

With the help of some fat yellow mice, scientists have discovered exactly how a mother's diet can permanently alter the functioning of genes in her offspring without changing the genes themselves.

The unusual strain of mouse carries a kind of trigger near the gene that determines not only the color of its coat but also its predisposition to obesity, diabetes and cancer. When pregnant mice were fed extra vitamins and supplements, the supplements interacted with the trigger in the fetal mice and shut down the gene. As a result, obese yellow mothers gave birth to standard brown baby mice that grew up lean and healthy.

Scientists have long known that what pregnant mothers eat—whether they are mice, fruit flies or humans—can profoundly affect the susceptibility of their offspring to disease. But until now they have not understood why, said

Dr. Randy Jirtle, a professor of radiation oncology at Duke and senior investigator of the study, which was reported in the Aug. 1 issue of *Molecular and Cellular Biology*.

The research is a milestone in the relatively new science of epigenetics, the study of how environmental factors like diet, stress and maternal nutrition can change gene function without altering the DNA sequence in any way.

Such factors have been shown to play a role in cancer, stroke, diabetes, schizophrenia, manic depression and other diseases as well as in shaping behavioral traits in offspring.

Most geneticists are focusing on sequences of genes in trying to understand which gene goes with which illness or behavior, said Dr. Thomas Insel, director of the National Institute of Mental Health. "But these epigenetic effects could turn out to be much more important. The field is revolutionary," he said, "and humbling."

Epigenetics may indeed hold answers to many mysteries that classical genetic approaches have been unable to solve, said Dr. Arturas Petronis, an associate professor of psychiatry at the Center for Addiction and Mental Health at the University of Toronto.

For example, why does one identical twin develop schizophrenia and not the other? Why do certain disease genes seem to affect or "penetrate" some people more than others? Why do complex diseases like autism turn up in more boys than girls?

For answers, epigeneticists are looking at biological mechanisms other than mutation that affect how genes function. One, called methylation, acts like a gas pedal or brake. It can turn gene expression up or down, on or off, depending on how much of it is around and what part of the genetic machinery it affects.

During methylation, a quartet of atoms called a methyl group attaches to a gene at a specific point and induces changes in the way the gene is expressed.

The process often inactivates genes not needed by a cell. The genes on one of the two X chromosomes in each female cell are silenced by methylation.

Methyl groups and other small molecules may sometimes attach to certain spots on chromosomes, helping to relax tightly coiled strands of DNA so that genes can be expressed.

Sometimes the coils are made tighter so that active genes are inactivated.

Methyl groups also inactivate remnants of past viral infections, called transposons. Forty percent of the human genome is made up of parasitic transposons.

Finally, methyl groups play a critical role in controlling genes involved in prenatal and postnatal development, including some 80 genes inherited from only one parent. Because these so-called imprinted genes must be methylated to function, they are vulnerable to diet and other environmental factors.

When a sperm and egg meet to form an embryo, each has a different pattern of methylated genes. The patterns are not passed on as genes are, but in a chemical battle of the sexes some of the egg and sperm patterns do seem to be inherited. In general, the egg seems to have the upper hand.

"We're compounds, mosaics of epigenetic patterns and gene sequences," said Dr. Arthur Beaudet, chairman of the molecular and human genetics department at Baylor College of Medicine in Houston. While DNA sequences are commonly compared to a text of written letters, he said, epigenetics is like the formatting in a word processing program.

Though the primary letters do not vary, the font can be large or small, Times Roman or Arial, italicized, bold, upper case, lower case, underlined or shadowed. They can be any color of the rainbow.

Methylation is nature's way of allowing environmental factors to tweak gene expression without making permanent mutations, Dr. Jirtle said.

Fleeting exposure to anything that influences methylation patterns during development can change the animal or person for a lifetime. Methyl groups are entirely derived from the foods people eat. And the effect may be good or bad. Maternal diet during pregnancy is consequently very important, but in ways that are not yet fully understood.

For his experiment, Dr. Jirtle chose a mouse that happens to have a transposon right next to the gene that codes for coat color. The transposon induces the gene to overproduce a protein that turns the mice pure yellow or mottled yellow and brown. The protein also blocks a feeding control center in the brain. Yellow mice therefore overeat and tend to develop diabetes and cancer.

To see if extra methylation would affect the mice, the researchers fed the animals a rich supply of methyl groups in supplements of vitamin B12, folic acid, choline and betaine from sugar beets just before they got pregnant and through the time of weaning their pups. The methyl groups silenced the transposon, Dr. Jirtle said, which in turn affected the adjacent coat color gene. The babies, born a normal brownish color, had an inherited predisposition to obesity, diabetes and cancer negated by maternal diet.

Unfortunately the scientists do not know which nutrient or combination of nutrients silence the genes, but noted that it did not take much. The animals were fed only three times as much of the supplements as found in a normal diet.

"If you looked at the mouse as a black box, you could say that adding these methyl-rich supplements to our diets might reduce our risk of obesity and cancer," Dr. Jirtle said. But, he added, there is strong reason for caution.

The positions of transposons in the human genome are completely different from the mouse pattern. Good maps of transposons in the human genome need to be made, he said. For that reason, it may be time to reassess the way the American diet is fortified with supplements, said Dr. Rob Waterland, a research fellow in Dr. Jirtle's lab and an expert on nutrition and epigenetics.

More than a decade ago, for example, epidemiological studies showed that some women who ate diets low in folic acid ran a higher risk of having babies with abnormalities in the spinal cord and brain, called neural tube defects.

To reduce this risk, folic acid was added to grains eaten by all Americans, and the incidence of neural tube defects fell substantially. But while there is no evidence that extra folic acid is harmful to the millions of people who eat fortified grains regularly, Dr. Waterland said, there is also no evidence that it is innocuous.

The worry is that excess folic acid may play a role in disorders like obesity or autism, which are on the rise, he said. Researchers are just beginning to study the question.

Epidemiological evidence shows that undernutrition and overnutrition in critical stages of development can lead to health problems in second and third generations, Dr. Waterland said.

A Dutch famine near the end of World War II led to an increased incidence of schizophrenia in adults who had been food-deprived during the first trimester of their mothers' pregnancy. Malnourishment among pregnant women in the South during the Civil War and the Depression has been proposed as an explanation for the high incidence of stroke among subsequent generations.

And the modern American diet, so full of fats and sugars, could be exerting epigenetic effects on future generations, positive or negative. Abnormal methylation patterns are a hallmark of most cancers, including colon, lung, prostate and breast cancer, said Dr. Peter Laird, an associate professor of biochemistry and molecular biology at the University of Southern California School of Medicine.

The anticancer properties attributed to many foods can be linked to nutrients, he said, as well as to the distinct methylation patterns of people who eat those foods. A number of drugs that inhibit methylation are now being tested as cancer treatments. Psychiatrists are also getting interested in the role of epigenetic factors in diseases like schizophrenia, Dr. Petronis said.

Methylation that occurs after birth may also shape such behavioral traits as fearfulness and confidence, said Dr. Michael Meaney, a professor of medicine and the director of the program for the study of behavior, genes and environment at McGill University in Montreal.

For reasons that are not well understood, methylation patterns are absent from very specific regions of the rat genome before birth. Twelve hours after rats are born, a new methylation pattern is formed. The mother rat then starts licking her pups. The first week is a critical period, Dr. Meaney said. Pups that are licked show decreased methylation patterns in an area of the brain that helps them handle stress. Faced with challenges later in life, they tend to be more confident and less fearful.

"We think licking affects a methylation enzyme that is ready and waiting for mother to start licking," Dr. Meaney said. In perilous times, mothers may be able to set the stress reactivity of their offspring by licking less. When there are fewer dangers around, the mothers may lick more.

CRITICAL THINKING QUESTIONS

1. This article discusses how environmental influences can alter the expression of a gene, while at the same time avoiding any DNA-sequence alterations. Why would natural selection fashion a mechanism in which the action of genes was strongly amenable to environmental input? Why might this be preferable to more permanent genetic change for some characteristics?

2. In the recent past, scientists have been able to clone animals, and there are currently business plans in place for the eventual cloning of beloved pets. What does this article suggest about the likelihood of getting another "perfect copy" of a favorite pet?

3

Genes, Environment, and Development

Influence of Life Stress on Depression: Moderation by a Polymorphism in the 5-HTT Gene

Avshalom Caspi, Karen Sugden, Terrie E. Moffitt, Alan Taylor, Ian W. Craig, HonaLee Harrington, Joseph McClay, Jonathan Mill, Judy Martin, Antony Braithwaite, and Richie Poulton

In a prospective-longitudinal study of a representative birth cohort, we tested why stressful experiences lead to depression in some people but not in others. A functional polymorphism in the promoter region of the serotonin transporter (5-HTT) gene was found to moderate the influence of stressful life events on depression. Individuals with one or two copies of the short allele of the 5-HTT promoter potymorphism exhibited more depressive symptoms, diagnosable depression, and suicidality in relation to stressful life events than individuals homozygous for the long allele. This epidemiological study thus provides evidence of a gene-by-environment interaction, in which an individual's response to environmental insults is moderated by his or her genetic makeup.

Reprinted (abstracted/excerpted) with permission from "Influence of life stress on depression: moderation by a polymorphism in the 5-HTT gene." (Reports). Avshalom Caspi; Karen Sugden; Terrie E. Moffitt; Alan Taylor; Ian W. Craig; HonaLee from Science, July 28, 2003 v. 301 i5631 p. 386 (4). Copyright 2003 AAAS.

Depression is among the top five leading causes of disability and disease burden throughout the world (1). Across the life span, stressful life events that involve threat, loss, humiliation, or defeat influence the onset and course of depression (2-5). However, not all people who encounter a stressful life experience succumb to its depressogenic effect. Diathesis-stress theories of depression predict that individuals' sensitivity to stressful events depends on their genetic makeup (6, 7). Behavioral genetics research supports this prediction, documenting that the risk of depression after a stressful event is elevated among people who are at high genetic risk and diminished among those at low genetic risk (8). However, whether specific genes exacerbate or buffer the effect of stressful life events on depression is unknown. In this study, a functional polymorphism in the promoter region of the serotonin transporter gene (SLC6A4) was used to characterize genetic vulnerability to depression and to test whether 5-HTT gene variation moderates the influence of life stress on depression.

The serotonin system provides a logical source of candidate genes for depression, because this system is the target of selective serotonin reuptake-inhibitor drugs that are effective in treating depression (9). The serotonin transporter has received particular attention because it is involved in the reuptake of serotonin at brain synapses (10). The promoter activity of the 5-HTT gene, located on 17q11.2, is modified by sequence elements within the proximal 5' regulatory region, designated the 5-HTT gene-linked polymorphic region (5-HTTLPR). The short ("s") allele in the 5-HTTLPR is associated with lower transcriptional efficiency of the promoter compared with the long ("1") allele (11).

Evidence for an association between the short promoter variant and depression is inconclusive (12). Although the 5-HTT gene may not be directly associated with depression, it could moderate the serotonergic response to stress. Three lines of experimental research suggest this hypothesis of a gene-by-environment (G x E) interaction. First, in mice with disrupted 5-HTT, homozygous and heterozygous (5-HTT $-/-$ and $+/-$) strains exhibited more fearful behavior and greater increases in the stress hormone (plasma) adrenocorticotropin in response to stress compared to homozygous (5-HTT $+/+$) controls, but in the absence of stress no differences related to genotype were observed (13). Second, in rhesus macaques, whose length variation of the 5-HTTLPR is analogous to that of humans, the short allele is associated with decreased serotonergic function [lower cerebrospinal fluid (CSF) 5-hydroxyindoleacetic acid concentrations] among monkeys reared in stressful conditions but not among normally reared monkeys (14). Third, human neuroimaging research suggests that the stress response is mediated by variations in the 5-HTTLPR. Humans with one or two copies of the s allele exhibit greater amygdala neuronal activity to fearful stimuli compared to individuals homozygous for the 1 allele (15). Taken together, these findings suggest the hypothesis that variations in the 5-HTT gene moderate psychopathological reactions to stressful experiences.

We tested this G x E hypothesis among members of the Dunedin Multi-disciplinary Health and Development Study (16). This representative birth cohort of 1037 children (52% male) has been assessed at ages 3, 5, 7, 9, 11, 13, 15, 18, and 21 and was virtually intact (96%) at the age of 26 years. A total of 847 Caucasian non-Maori study members, without stratification confounds, were divided into three groups on the basis of their 5-HTTLPR genotype (11): those with two copies of the s allele (s/s homozygotes; n = 147; 17%), those with one copy of the s allele (s/l heterozygotes; n = 435; 51%), and those with two copies of the l allele (l/l homozygotes; n = 265; 31%). There was no difference in genotype frequencies between the sexes [χ^2 (2) = 0.02, $P = 0.99$]. Stressful life events occurring after the 21st birthday and before the 26th birthday were assessed with the aid of a life-history calendar (17), a highly reliable method for ascertaining life-event histories (18). The 14 events included employment, financial, housing, health, and relationship stressors. Thirty percent of the study members experienced no stressful life events; 25% experienced one event; 20%, two events; 11%, three events; and 15%, four or more events. There were no significant differences between the three genotype groups in the number of life events they experienced, F(2,846) = 0.56, $P = 0.59$, suggesting that 5-HTTLPR genotype did not influence exposure to stressful life events.

Study members were assessed for past-year depression at age 26 with the use of the Diagnostic Interview Schedule (19), which yields a quantitative measure of depressive symptoms and a categorical diagnosis of a major depressive episode according to *Diagnostic and Statistical Manual of Mental Disorders* (DSM-IV) criteria (20). 17% of study members (58% female versus 42% male; odds ratio = 1.6; 95% confidence interval from 1.1 to 2.2) met criteria for a past-year major depressive episode, which is comparable to age and sex prevalence rates observed in U.S. epidemiological studies (21). In addition, 3% of the study members reported past-year suicide attempts or recurrent thoughts about suicide in the context of a depressive episode. We also collected informant reports about symptoms of depression for 96% of study members at age 26 by mailing a brief questionnaire to persons nominated by each study member as "someone who knows you well."

We used a moderated regression framework (22), with sex as a covariate, to test the association between depression and (i) 5-HTTLPR genotype, (ii) stressful life events, and (iii) their interaction (table S1). The interaction between 5-HTTLPR and life events showed that the effect of life events on self-reports of depression symptoms at age 26 was significantly stronger (P = 0.02) among individuals carrying an s allele than among l/l homozygotes (Fig. 1A) [Figure Omitted]. (All figures referenced can be found within the online version of this article, at http://www.infotrac-college.com.)

We further tested whether life events could predict within-individual increases in depression symptoms over time among individuals with an s allele by statistically controlling for the baseline number of depressive symptoms they had before the life events occurred (table S1). The significant interaction

(P = 0.05) showed that individuals carrying an s allele whose life events occurred after their 21st birthday experienced increases in depressive symptoms from the age of 21 to 26 years (b = 1.55, SE = 0.66, t = 2.35, P = 0.02 among s/s homozygotes and b = 1.25, SE = 0.34, t = 3.66, P < 0.001 among s/l heterozygotes) whereas l/l homozygotes did not (b = 0.17, SE = 0.41, t = 0.41, P = 0.68).

The G x E interaction also showed that stressful life events predicted a diagnosis of major depression among carriers of an s allele but not among l/l homozygotes (P = 0.056, Fig. 1B) [Figure Omitted]. We further tested whether life events could predict the onset of new diagnosed depression among carriers of an s allele (table S1). We excluded from analysis study members who were diagnosed with depression before age 21. The significant interaction (P = 0.02) showed that life events occurring after their 21st birthdays predicted depression at age 26 among carriers of an s allele who did not have a prior history of depression (b = 0.79, SE = 0.25, z = 3.16, P = 0.002 among s/s homozygotes and b = 0.41, SE = 0.12, z = 3.29, P = 0.001 among s/l heterozygotes) but did not predict onset of new depression among l/l homozygotes (b = 0.08, SE = 0.20, z = 0.42, P = 0.67). Further analyses showed that stressful life events predicted suicide ideation or attempt among individuals carrying an s allele but not among l/l homozygotes (P = 0.05, Fig. 1C [Figure Omitted]). The hypothesized G x E interaction was also significant when we predicted informant reports of age-26 depression (P < 0.01), an analysis that ruled out the possibility of self-report bias (Fig. 1D) [Figure Omitted]. The interaction showed that the effect of life events on informant reports of depression was stronger among individuals carrying an s allele than among l/l homozygotes. These analyses attest that the 5-HTT gene interacts with life events to predict depression symptoms, an increase in symptoms, depression diagnoses, new-onset diagnoses, suicidality, and an informant's report of depressed behavior.

This evidence that 5-HTTLPR variation moderates the effect of life events on depression does not constitute unambiguous evidence of a G x E interaction, because exposure to life events may be influenced by genetic factors; if individuals have a heritable tendency to enter situations where they encounter stressful life events, these events may simply be a genetically saturated marker (23, 24). Thus, what we have identified as a gene x environment interaction predicting depression could actually reflect a gene x "gene" interaction between the 5-HTTLPR and other genes we did not measure. We reasoned that, if our measure of life events represents merely genetic risk, then life events would interact with 5-HTTLPR even if they occurred after the depression episode. However, if our measure of life events represents environmental stress, then the timing of life events relative to depression must follow cause-effect order and life events that occur after depression should not interact with 5-HTTLPR to postdict depression. We tested this hypothesis by substituting the age-26 measure of depression with depression assessed in this longitudinal study when study members were 21 and 18 years old, before the occurrence of the measured life events between the ages of 21 and 26 years. Whereas the 5-HTTLPR x life events interaction predicted depression at the age of 26 years, this same interaction did not postdict depression reported at age 21 nor at the age of 18 years (table S2), indicating our finding is a true G x E interaction.

If 5-HTT genotype moderates the depressogenic influence of stressful life events, it should moderate the effect of life events that occurred not just in adulthood but also of stressful experiences that occurred in earlier developmental periods. Based on this hypothesis, we tested whether adult depression was predicted by the interaction between 5-HTTLPR and childhood maltreatment that occurred during the first decade of life (16, 25). Consistent with the G x E hypothesis, the longitudinal prediction from childhood maltreatment to adult depression was significantly moderated by 5-HTTLPR (table S3). The interaction showed (P = 0.05) that childhood maltreatment predicted adult depression only among individuals carrying an s allele but not among l/l homozygotes (Fig. 2) [Figure Omitted].

We previously showed that variations in the gene encoding the neuro-transmitter-metabolizing enzyme monoamine oxidase A (MAOA) moderate children's sensitivity to maltreatment (25). MAOA has high affinity for 5-HTT, raising the possibility that the protective effect of the l/l allele on psychiatric morbidity is further augmented by the presence of a genotype conferring high MAOA activity (13, 26). However, we found that the moderation of life stress on depression was specific to a polymorphism in the 5-HTT gene, because this effect was observed regardless of the individual's MAOA gene status (tables S4 and S5).

Until this study's findings are replicated, speculation about clinical implications is premature. Nonetheless, although carriers of an s 5-HTTLPR allele who experienced four or more life events constituted only 10% of the birth cohort, they accounted for almost one-quarter (23%) of the 133 cases of diagnosed depression. Moreover, among cohort members suffering four or more stressful life events, 33% of individuals with an s allele became depressed, whereas only 17% of the l/l homozygotes developed depression (Fig. 3) [Figure Omitted]. Thus, the G x E's attributable risk and predictive sensitivity indicate that more knowledge about the functional properties of the 5-HTT gene may lead to better pharmacological treatments for those already depressed. Although the short 5-HTTLPR variant is too prevalent for discriminatory screening (over half of the Caucasian population has an s allele), a microarray of genes might eventually identify those needing prophylaxis against life's stressful events (27).

Evidence of a direct relation between the 5-HTTLPR and depression has been inconsistent (12), perhaps because prior studies have not considered participants' stress histories. In this study, no direct association between the 5-HTT gene and depression was observed. Previous experimental paradigms, including 5-HTT knockout mice (13), stress-reared rhesus macaques (14), and human functional neuroimaging (15), have shown that the 5-HTT gene can interact with environmental conditions, although these experiments did not address depression. Our study demonstrates that this G x E interaction extends to the natural development of depression in a representative sample of humans. However, we could not test hypotheses about brain endophenotypes (28) intermediate between the 5-HTT gene and depression be cause of the difficulty of taking CSF or functional magnetic resonance imaging measurements in an epidemiological cohort.

Much genetic research has been guided by the assumption that genes cause diseases, but the expectation that direct paths will be found from gene to disease has not proven fruitful for complex psychiatric disorders (29). Our findings of G x E interaction for the 5-HTT gene and another candidate gene, MAOA (25), point to a different, evolutionary model. This model assumes that genetic variants maintained at high prevalence in the population probably act to promote organisms' resistance to environmental pathogens (30). We extend the concept of environmental pathogens to include traumatic, stressful life experiences and propose that the effects of genes may be uncovered when such pathogens are measured (in naturalistic studies) or manipulated (in experimental studies). To date, few linkage studies detect genes, many candidate gene studies fail consistent replication, and genes that replicate account for little variation in the phenotype (29). If replicated, our G x E findings will have implications for improving research in psychiatric genetics. Incomplete gene penetrance, a major source of error in linkage pedigrees, can be explained if a gene's effects are expressed only among family members exposed to environmental risk. If risk exposure differs between samples, candidate genes may fail replication. If risk exposure differs among participants within a sample, genes may account for little variation in the phenotype. We speculate that some multifactorial disorders, instead of resulting from variations in many genes of small effect, may result from variations in fewer genes whose effects are conditional on exposure to environmental risks.

CRITICAL THINKING QUESTIONS

1. According to this article, people who carry one or two copies of a short allele on the 5-HTT gene are more likely to suffer from depression. By contrast, those individuals with at least one copy of the long allele on the same gene do not appear to be as prone to depression. However, these differences emerge *only* when individuals are exposed to stressful life events. Does this mean that carriers of the 5-HTT short variant are more sensitive to environmental influences than carriers of the long variant? Explain why or why not.

2. "Penetrance" is a term used by geneticists to describe the probability of a given trait being expressed when an individual carries the corresponding genotype. Caspi et al. state that their paper has implications for the examination of "incomplete penetrance." Explain why this is the case.

3. Often times, researchers interested in the precursors to diseases (such as major depression) identify affected individuals, and then ask them to reflect upon past experiences. Researchers then compare the affected individuals' responses to the responses of unaffected individuals asked the same questions. By contrast, Caspi et al. followed research participants longitudinally, *before* they had actually developed depression. Why might this be a more accurate way to investigate precursors to disease than participants' retrospective accounts, particularly for a disease such as depression?

REFERENCES AND NOTES

1. C. J. Tang, A. D. Lopez, *Lancet 349*, 1498 (1997).

2. G. W. Brown, *Soc. Psychiatry Psychiatr. Epidemiol. 33*, 363 (1998).

3. K. S. Kendler, L. M. Karkowski, C. A. Prescott, *Am. J. Psychiatry 156*, 837 (1999).

4. R. C. Kessler, *Annu. Rev. Psychol. 48*, 191 (1997).

5. D. S. Pine, P. Cohen, J. G. Johnson, J. S. Brook, *J. Affect. Disorders 68*, 49 (2002).

6. E. J. Costello et al., *Biol. Psychiatry 52*, 529 (2002).

7. S. M. Monroe, A. D. Simons, *Psychol. Bull. 110*, 406 (1991).

8. K. S. Kendler et al., *Am. J. Psychiatry 152*, 833 (1995).

9. C.A. Tamminga et al., *Biol. Psychiatry 52*, 589 (2002).

10. K. P. Lesch, M. D. Greenberg, J. D. Higley, A. Bennett, D. L. Murphy, in *Molecular Genetics and the Human Personality*, J. Benjamin, R. P. Ebstein, R. H. Belmaker, Eds. [American Psychiatric Association (APA), Washington, DC, 2002], pp. 109–136.

11. K. P. Lesch et al., *Science 274*, 1527 (1996).

12. K. P. Lesch, in *Behavioral Genetics in the Postgenomics Era*, R. Plomin, J. C. DeFries, I. W. Craig, P. McGuffin, Eds. (APA, Washington, DC, 2003), pp. 389–424.

13. D. L. Murphy et al., *Brain Res. Bull. 56*, 487 (2001).

14. A. J. Bennett et al., *Mol. Psychiatry 7*, 188 (2002).

15. A. R. Hariri et al., *Science 297*, 400 (2002).

16. Materials and methods are available as supporting material on Science Online.

17. A. Caspi et al., *Int. J. Methods Psychiatr. Res. 6*, 101 (1996).

18. R. F. Belli, W. L. Shay, F. P. Stafford, *Public Opin. Q. 6s*, 4s (2001).

19. L. N. Robins, L. Cottler, K. Bucholtz, W. Compton, *Diagnostic Interview Schedule for DSM-IV* (Washington University, St. Louis, MO, 1995).

20. APA, *Diagnostic and Statistical Manual of Mental Disorders* (APA, Washington, DC, ed. 4, 1994).

21. R. C. Kessler, K. A. McGonagle, M. Swartz, D. G. Blazer, C. B. Nelson, *J. Affect. Disorders 29,* 85 (1993).

22. L. S. Aiken, S. G. West, *Multiple Regression: Testing and Interpreting Interactions* (Sage, Thousand Oaks, CA, 1991).

23. K. S. Kendler, L. Karkowski-Shuman, *Psychol. Med. 27,* 539 (1997).

24. R. Plomin, C. S. Bergeman, *Behav. Brain Sci. 14,* 373 (1991).

25. A. Caspi et al., *Science 297,* 851 (2002).

26. N. Satichon et al., *J. Neurosci. 21,* 884 (2001).

27. W. E. Evans, M. V. Relling, *Science 286,* 487 (1999).

28. I. I. Gottesman, T. D. Gould, *Am. J. Psychiatry 160,* 636 (2003).

29. D. Hamer, *Science 298,* 71 (2002).

30. A. V. S. Hill, *Br. Med. Bull. 55,* 401 (1999).

31. We thank P. Silva, founder of the Dunedin Multidisciplinary Health and Development Study, Air New Zealand, and the study members, their families, and their friends. Supported by the Health Research Council of New Zealand and the University of Wisconsin Graduate School and by grants from the U.K. Medical Research Council, the William T. Grant Foundation, and the U.S. National institute of Mental Health (MH49414 and MH45070). T.E.M. is a Royal Society–Wolfson Research Merit Award holder. The study protocol was approved by the institutional review boards of the participating universities.

SUPPORTING ONLINE MATERIAL

www.sciencemag.org/cgi/content/full/301/5631/386/ DC1 Materials and Methods Tables S1 to S5

Avshalom Caspi, (1,2) Karen Sugden, (1) Terrie E. Moffitt, (1,2)★ Alan Taylor, (1) Ian W. Craig, (1) HonaLee Harrington, (2) Joseph McClay, (1) Jonathan Mill, (1) Judy Martin, (3) Antony Braithwaite, (4) Richie Poulton (3)

(1) Medical Research Council Social Genetic, and Developmental Psychiatry Research Centre, institute of Psychiatry, King's College London, PO80 De Crespigny Park, London, SE5 8AF, UK. (2) Department of Psychology, University of Wisconsin, Madison, WI 53706, USA. (3) Dunedin School of Medicine, (4) Department of Pathology, University of Otago, Dunedin, New Zealand.

★To whom correspondence should be addressed. E-mail: t.moffitt@iop.kcl.ac.uk

4

Prenatal Development and Birth

Effects of Paternal Exposure to Alcohol on Offspring Development: Paternal Alcohol Consumption May Affect Fetal Development Through a Direct Effect on the Father's Sperm or Gonads

Theodore J. Cicero

Researchers have been attempting to isolate factors that cause alcoholism in male children whose biological fathers are alcoholics. Some studies have established this connection, but further research in genetic linkage would be beneficial to show which genes can cause diseases.

Alcohol Health & Research World, Wntr 1994, v18 n1 p37(5).

"Effects of Paternal Exposure to Alcohol on Offspring Development: Paternal Alcohol Consumption May Affect Fetal Development Through a Direct Effect on the Father's Sperm or Gonads" by Theodore J. Cicero. © 1994 U.S. Government Printing Office.

Paternal alcohol consumption may affect fetal development through a direct effect on the father's sperm or gonads. This possibility casts new light on the heritability of alcoholism in humans.

The adverse consequences of maternal alcohol intake during pregnancy on fetal outcome are well documented (for a review, see Meyer and Riley 1986). However, the possibility that paternal alcohol consumption also may induce deficits in the progeny has received relatively little attention. This is somewhat surprising, as alcoholism appears to be linked genetically with the father in humans (Merikangas 1990; Pickens et al. 1991), and studies indicate that male offspring of alcoholic fathers have behavioral problems and impaired intellectual skills as well as hormonal and nervous system anomalies (see below).

This article discusses the possible direct effects of paternal alcohol consumption on fetal development, distinguishing these effects from studies of the genetic heritability of alcoholism. The article also discusses the possibility that such paternal effects may contribute to cognitive and biochemical disturbances that may be associated with altered responses to alcohol that might lead to addiction.

For purposes of this review, alcoholism is broadly defined as the excessive and repetitive consumption of alcohol that results in significant disturbances in a person's life, such as preoccupation with drinking to the exclusion of other activities, inability to perform adequately at work, and deterioration of family or other social interactions. In general, the study populations discussed below meet not only these criteria but also others required for a clinical diagnosis of alcoholism.

DEFICITS IN THE OFFSPRING
OF MALE ALCOHOLICS

Many studies have indicated that children of alcoholic fathers often demonstrate impaired cognitive(1) skills and are more likely to be hyperactive than are children of nonalcoholic biological parents (Hegedus et al. 1984; Tartar et al. 1989). These studies generally adopted controls to ensure that the effects were not due to such factors as maternal drug use, socioeconomic variables, race, and psychiatric or medical disorders in the parents. These effects also were observed in children borne of alcoholic biological fathers but raised by nonalcoholic adoptive parents.

Sons of alcoholics also have abnormal electrical activity in the brain as measured by the electroencephalograph (EEG) (Begleiter and Projesz 1988; Ehlers et al. 1989; Schuckit et al. 1987a). Moreover, it has been shown that the sons of alcoholics, when compared with sons of nonalcoholic parents, demonstrate abnormal hormonal responses to short-term administration of alcohol (Schuckit 1988; Schuckit et al. 1987 a,b, 1988). Hence, these data seem to suggest that genetic factors of the biological fathers that relate to their drinking behavior may have a significant effect on the intellectual and behavioral development of their offspring.

GENETIC BASIS FOR TRANSMISSION
OF ALCOHOLISM

The foregoing studies generally represent attempts to identify markers for the predisposition for alcoholism. A marker can most easily be understood as a specific trait that may predict whether a person is at risk for developing a medical disorder. For example, blood tests can be used to predict the occurrence of various genetic disorders, including cystic fibrosis and Down syndrome. Researchers are attempting to identify markers that could serve as early indicators of potential susceptibility to alcoholism.

Genetic linkage studies are a more useful approach for identifying a genetic basis for alcoholism. These sophisticated molecular biological techniques attempt to establish causal links between disorders and specific genes. Using these techniques, researchers have identified genes responsible for at least some types of Alzheimer's disease, cystic fibrosis, and other genetically transmissible disorders. The discovery of an association between a medical disorder and a specific gene provides a better understanding of the mechanisms underlying the disorder and may therefore provide a basis for improved treatment.

In the case of alcoholism, genetic linkage studies have produced equivocal results. This is not surprising, as the heterogeneous nature of alcoholism is not likely to be explained by a single gene. Furthermore, the results of linkage studies depend heavily on the specific criteria used to define alcoholism in the subject population and the control populations with which they are compared. Most such studies have used widely varying sets of criteria, making comparisons between studies difficult.

Twin and Adoptee Studies

Results of twin and adoptee studies are consistent with a genetic predisposition to the development of alcoholism. These studies have demonstrated that sons borne of alcoholic biological fathers and raised by nonalcoholic fathers are at much greater risk for developing alcoholism than are sons of nonalcoholics raised by either alcoholic or nonalcoholic fathers (for reviews, see Cloninger et al. 1989; Merikangas 1990; Pickens et al. 1991). Perhaps most importantly, these studies demonstrate that the drinking history of the stepfather is irrelevant in terms of the development of alcoholism in sons borne of either alcoholic or nonalcoholic biological fathers. Sons of nonalcoholic biological fathers had the same incidence of alcoholism as in the general population, whereas sons of alcoholic biological fathers seemed to have a higher incidence of alcoholism irrespective of how they were raised.

Twin and adoptee studies are useful for establishing a familial or genetic basis for alcoholism, but they are limited in scope. Thus, it has not been possible to distinguish completely between environmental and biological factors in the development of alcoholism. Nevertheless, the studies discussed in this and previous sections suggest that there is a high incidence of alcoholism in the offspring of alcoholic fathers and that these offspring can be clearly distinguished from children of nonalcoholics in several ways.

Alcoholic Mothers and Daughters

As a result of the studies discussed above, it has been widely assumed that alcoholism is genetically transmissible only in males. These results may simply reflect the relatively low incidence of alcoholism in females compared with males (e.g., Cloninger et al. 1989). However, the diagnosis of alcoholism is being made in increasing numbers of women (Johnston et al. 1987), contradicting the earlier belief that alcoholism affects only males. (2) Further studies are needed to more firmly establish whether the daughters of alcoholic fathers have any higher risk for developing alcohol-related problems than daughters born of nonalcoholic parents.

In addition, not all studies have adequately considered the role of maternal alcoholism or abuse of other drugs; given the established linkage between prenatal alcohol consumption and developmental anomalies such as FAS, for example, these factors must be rigorously controlled for in such experiments. Another question that has been largely ignored is whether the mother's drinking behavior can influence alcohol consumption patterns in their offspring independently of the drinking habits of the biological fathers or stepfathers.

STUDIES IN ANIMAL MODELS

As discussed above, numerous studies clearly suggest impairments in the sons of alcoholic fathers. However, two important questions cannot be conclusively addressed in studies with humans: Are the observed deficits due to biological or to social determinants? Do these deficits represent the toxic effects of alcohol per se or the genetic transmission of specific traits? The use of an animal model permits a direct assessment of whether the paternal consumption of alcohol is a potential toxicant to the developing fetus. Although no animal model could duplicate the complex psychosocial factors that contribute to alcoholism in humans, such models can be extremely helpful in elucidating the biological aspects of alcoholism.

Teratogenic Effects of Alcohol

The initial reports of infant malformations and mortality resulting from paternal alcohol consumption in animals appeared more than 70 years ago (Stockard and Papanicolaou 1916, 1918a, b). These studies demonstrated profound alcohol–induced reductions in fertility, gross developmental abnormalities, and considerable levels of infant mortality. These results were initially dismissed, largely on the grounds that if these massive deficits in animals had clinical significance, they would already have been observed in humans. Another view held that as a clear-cut mechanism for these effects could not be demonstrated, the effects themselves must not exist. Moreover, several attempts to replicate these results were unsuccessful (MacDowell et al. 1926; Durham and Woods 1932).

Renewed interest in the effects of paternal drug administration emerged approximately 15 years ago as a result of studies in animal models showing that alcohol influences male sexual performance and fertility, the viability of offspring, and maturation of the fetus and newborn (for a review, see Abel 1992). These effects appeared to be qualitatively and quantitatively different from those observed in FAS. However, a few reports suggested that FAS could occur in offspring of alcoholic fathers with no evidence of heavy alcohol consumption during pregnancy by the mother (Scheiner et al. 1979; Henderson et al. 1981; Randall and Noble 1980). It remains to be resolved whether the anomalies observed in the offspring of fathers exposed to alcohol are characteristic of FAS or some other syndrome. Nevertheless, it seems clear that paternal, pregestational alcohol administration can produce adverse effects in the offspring, at least under the conditions of these early studies.

Unfortunately, methodological problems in this research have made comparisons between studies difficult and definitive conclusions nearly impossible. These problems include very limited numbers of experimental subjects; inappropriate modes of alcohol administration, causing problems with nutrition and stress; variation in the length of alcohol exposure among studies; and whether or not a drug-free interval was provided prior to mating. Moreover, some recent studies, using appropriate alcohol administration regimens and adequate control groups, failed to observe any gross anomalies characteristic of FAS such as were observed in some earlier studies.

Specific Deficits in the Offspring of Alcoholic Fathers

More recently, we and others have examined the influence of paternal alcohol consumption on offspring under well-controlled conditions in animal models (Cicero et al. 1991b; Wozniak et al. 1991; Abel 1989, 1992; Abel and Lee 1988; Abel and Moore 1987; Abel and Tan 1988; Berk et al. 1989).

Deficits in Puberty and Sexual Maturation. Initially, we focused on the effects of alcohol on puberty and sexual maturation, because alcoholism and alcohol use are increasing among adolescents (Johnston et al. 1987). We found that alcohol administered to prepubescent male rats significantly affected many primary indicators of puberty and sexual maturation as those rats developed. The alcohol diet was terminated when the animals were sexually mature; all reproductive hormonal indicators then quickly recovered, becoming indistinguishable from non–alcohol–fed control animals 2 to 3 weeks after termination of alcohol exposure. In contrast to these results obtained in immature rats, the effects of alcohol on reproductive hormones in the fully mature animal were transitory and of considerably lesser magnitude.

To confirm that the effects of preadolescent exposure to alcohol on reproductive hormones were fully reversible, we mated alcohol-exposed adolescent male rats, in which the effects of alcohol on reproductive hormones had apparently completely dissipated (2 to 3 weeks after termination of alcohol exposure), with drug-naive females. We examined sexual behavior, capacity to mate, and the ability to conceive healthy litters in alcohol-exposed male rats compared with controls. We also examined relatively crude indices of the development of their offspring ("alcohol-sired" rats).

Although pregnancy rates were essentially equivalent when alcohol-exposed and control animals were mated with drug-naive females, the size of the litters was modestly but significantly smaller with the alcohol-exposed males. However, in other respects, such as birth weights, ratio of males to females, mortality rates, and gross developmental features, alcohol-sired offspring were identical with controls. Taken together, the results of the above experiments show that early exposure to alcohol adversely affects puberty and sexual maturation, with essentially complete recovery of reproductive function occurring within 2 to 3 weeks after alcohol withdrawal.

Offspring Effects. We more fully characterized the development of the offspring of alcohol-exposed and control animals to determine whether more subtle differences might exist. We found significant disturbances in hormonal function in adult alcohol-sired rats compared with offspring sired by normal male rats. For example, male alcohol-sired offspring had significantly lower levels of testosterone and beta-endorphin as well as lighter seminal vesicles. (3) We were unable to demonstrate any impairment in reproductive hormone function in female alcohol-sired offspring. However, we found that female— but not male—alcohol-sired offspring had abnormal baseline levels of certain stress-related hormones and responded differently to stress than did control female offspring.

The alcohol-sired offspring in these tests did not differ from controls in terms of body weights measured at various times during development, the appearance of various developmental landmarks, or performance on several developmental tests. However, the adult alcohol-sired males performed poorly on several spatial learning tests; other forms of learning appeared to be relatively unaffected. Female alcohol-sired offspring displayed no significant learning impairments on any test we employed.

Thus, our results indicate pronounced gender-specific hormonal function and behavioral defects in the offspring of fathers exposed to alcohol as adolescents. Perhaps of equal importance, the deficits we observed in alcohol-sired offspring appeared to be selective. We observed no differences in several hormonal systems other than those associated with reproductive hormones and stress nor were there differences on a variety of behavioral tests other than those relying on spatial learning. This selectivity might account for previous reports in which no gross developmental anomalies were observed to result from paternal alcohol exposure.

In addition, these results are highly consistent with the observations in humans, in that offspring of alcoholic fathers, as opposed to offspring suffering from FAS, are not grossly malformed or impaired but have pronounced selective intellectual and functional deficits. Thus, our animal model may prove to be useful for examining deficits derived from paternal alcohol exposure in offspring of human alcoholics.

We are unaware of any reports examining the effects of paternal drug administration using an experimental design similar to the one we used in our studies. However, several researchers have reported that exposure of fully mature male rats to environmental toxicants and drugs, including alcohol, can lead to numerous behavioral, biochemical, and hormonal disturbances in their offspring (for reviews, see Cohen 1986; Joffe and Soyka 1982; Narod et al. 1988). For example, Abel (1989, 1992) found that alcohol administration to male rodents adversely affects the hormonal and cognitive status of the offspring.

Although many studies have reported deficits in alcohol-sired offspring, earlier researchers studied only adult animals and used extremely high doses of toxicants or drugs. Moreover, alcohol exposure continued through conception, and the appearance or functional activity of the sperm was often grossly altered. Many of these studies do not permit a distinction between the chronic effects of alcohol and its acute toxicity with respect to reproductive hormonal function.

In our ongoing studies, we have shown that a period of moderate exposure of the father to alcohol during sexual maturation, followed by a drug-free period sufficient to restore normal hormonal status, resulted in the abnormal development of both male and female offspring. Thus, our results presumably do not reflect the acute effects of alcohol or the consequences of withdrawal but rather some residual effect of early exposure to alcohol during development of the future father. Consequently, the experimental design used in our studies may be useful for examining the possible consequences of heavy alcohol use by human male adolescents on the development of the offspring they bear later as adults.

Mechanisms of Paternal-Alcohol Effects on Offspring

The mechanisms underlying the deficits observed in alcohol-sired animal offspring are not easily explained. It is, however, clear that the results observed in our studies are due exclusively to paternal alcohol exposure, because they cannot reasonably be ascribed to the female. Specifically, the females were drug naive and matched to control animals in terms of their previous capacity to deliver and nurture healthy litters. Moreover, their offspring developed normally with no evidence of fetal mortality, and post mortem evaluation revealed no clinically significant problems in the females that could account for any of the observed effects.

There are three possible mechanisms for the effect of paternal alcohol consumption on the offspring. First, alcohol may directly affect the characteristics and properties of sperm, perhaps by causing mutations in the sperm's genetic material. Second, sperm may be "selected" in some way such that only a specific population is functionally intact following prolonged exposure to alcohol. Third, alcohol consumption might alter the chemical composition of semen so as to influence the activity of ejaculated sperm.

In this connection, several recent studies have shown that various drugs, including alcohol, may induce subtle mutations in sperm (Obe et al. 1986; Narod et al. 1988), and long-term alcohol exposure may result in gross abnormalities in the appearance and motility of sperm (for a review, see Abel 1992). In addition, it has been demonstrated that drugs and toxicants accumulate in semen (e.g., Yazigi et al. 1991), and some drugs, such as cocaine, may bind to the sperm surface (Yazigi et al. 1991).

These data suggest that drugs may either impair sperm directly, thereby influencing the development of offspring, or be transported to the ovum via the seminal fluid by physically binding to sperm. Alternatively, alcohol might alter the biochemical and nutritional composition of the seminal fluid, which is necessary for the survival of sperm and to ensure successful conception. If the latter is true, then it can be postulated that the embryo may be exposed to high levels of a toxicant or that seminal substances necessary for facilitating and maintaining the embryo are altered during the earliest stages of development, adversely affecting normal maturation. These possibilities are pure conjecture, as a causal link with birth defects has not been established.

It may be significant that endogenous opioids are synthesized in the testes. Endogenous opioids are morphinelike substances, best known as chemical messengers in the brain. Their functions are not clearly understood, but they generally involve modulation of hormonal systems. Endogenous opioids carry out their functions by binding to specific receptor proteins embedded in the surfaces of cells, thereby ultimately causing chemical changes to occur within those cells. Receptors for endogenous opioids have been found to occur in certain testicular cells and on the surface of sperm.

Therefore, these substances may play a significant role in modulating the production of sex hormones and sperm in the testicles. Although the effects of alcohol on testicular endogenous opioid function are unknown, both short- and long-term alcohol use significantly affect endogenous opioid systems in the brain and other organs.

Alcohol and morphine have similar effects on puberty and sexual maturation (Cicero et al. 1991a), and the results of breeding animals exposed to morphine during adolescence with drug-naive females were similar to those observed in animals exposed to alcohol. For example, morphine-sired male offspring had lower serum testosterone and other hormone levels, lower weights of the seminal vesicles, and heavier adrenal glands.[4] Female morphine-derived adult offspring had significantly higher levels of adrenal stress-related hormones in the blood.

Moreover, Friedler and associates (Friedler 1985; Friedler and Cicero 1988) have demonstrated cognitive deficits in the offspring of morphine-exposed males mated with drug-naive females, similar in some respects to those observed in the offspring of alcohol-exposed males. These similarities between two commonly used drugs, alcohol and opiates, raise several interesting questions, such as whether these drugs act through a common pathway and whether other drugs likely to be used during adolescence would produce similar effects.

CONCLUSIONS

Alcohol consumption by male rats appears to have long-lasting effects on their ability to produce normal progeny. Studies suggest that alcohol itself may be a direct toxicant to sperm, inducing subtle yet marked deficits in the offspring of alcohol-exposed fathers. If true, this will require a reassessment of the numerous studies in humans examining the heritability of specific traits predisposing the offspring to alcoholism. Specifically, it has been assumed that the sons of alcoholics inherit some genetic trait that predisposes them to alcoholism, but few investigators have considered the possibility that these deficits could be due to alcohol's being a direct gonadal toxicant or teratogenic agent.

Results relative to the paternal effects of alcohol on progeny are still in a very early stage of development. A concerted effort must be made to replicate these findings and to address other important issues, such as: How much alcohol must fathers drink to produce deficits in their offspring? Are the effects observed in the offspring of alcohol-exposed fathers transmitted from one generation to the next? Can these effects be reversed by long-term abstinence of the father prior to conception?

Whereas the paternal effects of alcohol on both male and female offspring appear to be pronounced, no studies as yet suggest that any of the deficits observed in animal models are causally related to the development of alcoholism. Studies are needed to determine whether the observed cognitive and biochemical disturbances are associated with altered responses to alcohol that might lead to addiction. Such studies would also help determine whether animal models are appropriate for examining the causal factors and heritability of alcoholism in humans.

Theodore J. Cicreo, PhD., is professor of neuropharmacology in the Department of Psychiatry, Washington University School of Medicine, St. Louis, Missouri.

This work was supported by grants AA07144 and AA07466 from the National Institute on Alcohol Abuse and Alcoholism and by Research Scientist Award DA00095 and grant DA03833 from the National Institute on Drug Abuse.

NOTES

(1) Cognition refers to intellectual functions such as information processing, learning, and memory. (2) Editor's Note: For more information on the role of genetic factors in the etiology of alcoholism of women, see Kendler, K.S.;

Heath, A.C.; Neale, M.C.; Kessler, R.C.; and Eaves, L.J. Population-based twin study of alcoholism in women. *Journal of the American Medical Association* 268(14):1877–1882, 1992. (3) Testosterone is the primary male sex hormone; beta-endorphin is a hormonelike substance in the brain, belonging to the class of endogenous peptides; and the seminal vesicles are sperm-producing tubular structures in the testes. (4) The adrenal glands, located above the kidneys, produce hormones that help regulate various metabolic functions and the response to stress.

CRITICAL THINKING QUESTIONS

1. Children born to alcoholic fathers are more likely to become alcoholics themselves. This is true whether or not they are raised by their own or by adoptive parents. What are the implications of finding elevated rates of alcoholism for children of alcoholic fathers despite different family environments?

2. Cicero states that previous studies on the effects of paternal alcohol use continued alcohol exposure through conception. Why did he believe it was important to discontinue paternal alcohol use prior to conception in his study? How does this relate to his specific research question?

3. Given the knowledge that children born to alcoholic fathers are more likely to become alcoholics themselves, should prospective adoptive parents be told of a potential adoptee's higher risk of developing alcoholism given family history? Would this be ethical? Why or why not?

REFERENCES

Abel, E.L. Paternal and maternal alcohol consumption: Effects on offspring in two strains of rats. *Alcoholism: Clinical and Experimental Research* 13:533–541, 1989.

Abel, E.L. Paternal exposure to alcohol. In: Sonderegger, T.B., ed. *Perinatal Substance Abuse: Research Findings* and Clinical Implications. Baltimore: Johns Hopkins University Press, 1992. pp.132–162.

Abel, E.L., and Lee, J.A. Paternal alcohol exposure affects offspring behavior but not body or organ weights in mice. *Alcoholism: Clinical and Experimental Research* 12:349–355, 1988.

Abel, E.L., and Moore, C. Effects of paternal alcohol consumption in mice. *Alcoholism: Clinical and Experimental Research* 11:533–535, 1987.

Abel, E.L., and Tan, S.E. Effects of paternal alcohol consumption on pregnancy outcome in rats. *Neurotoxicology and Teratology* 19:187–192, 1988.

Begleiter, H., and Projesz, B. Potential biological markers in individuals at high risk for developing alcoholism. *Alcoholism: Clinical and Experimental Research* 12:488–493, 1988.

Berk, R.S.; Montgomery, I.N.; Hazlett, L.D.; and Abel, E.L. Paternal alcohol consumption: Effect on ocular response and serum antibody response to Pseudomonas aeruginosa infection in offspring. *Alcoholism: Clinical and Experimental Research* 13:795–798, 1989.

Cicero, T.J; Adams, M.L.; Giordano, A.; Miller, B.T.; O'Connor, L.; and Nock, B. Influence of morphine exposure during adolescence on the sexual maturation of male rats and the development of their offspring. *Journal of Pharmacology and Experimental Therapeutics* 256:1086–1093, 1991a.

Cicero, T.J.; Adams, M.L.; O'Connor, L.H.; Nock, B.; Meyer, E.R.; and Wozniak, D. Influence of chronic alcohol administration on representative indices of puberty and sexual maturation in male rats and the development of their progeny. *Journal of Pharmacology and Experimental Therapeutics* 255: 707–715, 1991b.

Cloninger, C.R.; Sigvardsson, S.; Gilligan, S.B.; von Knorring, A.L.; Reich, T.; and Bohman, M. Genetic heterogeneity and the classification of alcoholism. *Advances in Alcohol and Substance Abuse* 7(3/4):3–16, 1989.

Cohen, F.L. Paternal contributions to birth defects. *Nursing Clinics of North America* 21:49–64, 1986.

Durham, F.M., and Woods, H.M. Alcohol and Inheritance: An Experimental Study. Medical Research Council Special Reports Series. No. 168. London: H.M.S.O., 1932.

Ehlers, C.L.; Wall, T.L.; and Schuckit, M.A. EEG spectral characteristics following ethanol administration in young men. *Electroencephalography and Clinical Neurophysiology* 73:179–187, 1989.

Friedlier, G. Effects of limited paternal exposure to xenobiotic agents on the development of progeny. *Neurobehavioral Toxicology and Teratology* 7:739–743, 1985.

Friedlier, G., and Cicero, T.J. Paternal pregestational opiate exposure in male mice: Neuroendocrine deficits in their offspring. *Substance Abuse* 8:109–116, 1988.

Hegedus, A.M.; Alterman, A.I.; and Tarter, R.E. Learning achievement in sons of alcoholics. *Alcoholism: Clinical and Experimental Research* 8:330–333, 1984.

Henderson, G.I.; Patwardhan, R.V.; Joyumpa, A.M.; and Schenker, S. Fetal alcohol syndrome: Overview of pathogenesis. *Neurobehavioral Toxicology and Teratology* 3:73–80, 1981.

Joffe, J.M., and Soyka, L.F. Paternal drug exposure: Effects on reproduction and progeny. *Seminars in Permatology* 6:116–124, 1982.

Johnston, L.P.; O'Mally, P.M.; and Bachman, J.G. National Trends in Drug Abuse and Related Factors Among American High School Students and Young Adults, 1975–1986. National Institute on Drug Abuse. DHHS Pub. No. (ADM)87–1535. Washington, DC: Supt. of Docs., U.S. Govt. Print. Off., 1987.

C.G. Heavy alcoholization and prenatal mortality in mice. *Proceedings of the Society for Experimental Biology and Medicine* 23:652–654, 1926.

Merikangas, K.R. The genetic epidemiology of alcoholism. *Psychological Medicine* 20:11–22, 1990.

Meyer, L.S., and Filey, E.P. Behavioral teratology of alcohol. In: Riley, E.P., and Vorhees, C.V., eds. *Handbook of Behavioral Teratology*. New York: Plenum Press, 1986. pp. 101–134.

Narod, S.A.; Douglas, G.E.; Nesmann, E.R.; and Blakey, D.H. Human mutagens: Evidence from paternal exposure. *Environmental and Molecular Mutagenesis* 11:401–415, 1988.

Obe, G.; Ristow, H.; and Herha, J. Effect of ethanol on chromosomal structure and function. In: Majchrowicz, E., and Noble, E.P., eds. *Biochemistry and Pharmacology of Ethanol*. Vol. 1. New York: Plenum Press, 1986. pp. 659–676.

Pickens, R.W; Svikis, D.S.; McGue, M.; Lykken, D.T.; Heston, L.L.; and Clayton, P.J. Heterogeneity in the inheritance of alcoholism. *Archives of General Psychiatry* 48(1):19–28, 1991.

Randall, C.L., and Noble, E.P. Alcohol abuse and fetal growth in development. In: Mello, N.K., ed. *Advances in Substance Abuse*. Vol. 1. Greenwich, CT: JAI Press, 1980. pp. 327–367.

Scheiner, A.P.; Donovan, C.M.; and Bartoshesky, L.E. Fetal alcohol syndrome in child whose parents had stopped drinking. *Lancet* 1(8125):1077–1078, 1979.

Schuckit, M.A. Reactions to alcohol in sons of alcoholies and controls. *Alcoholism: Clinical and Experimental Research* 12:465–470, 1988.

Schuckit, M.A.; Butters, N.; Lyn, L.; and Irwin, M. Neuropsychologic deficits and the risk for alcoholism. *Neuropsychopharmacology* 1:45–53, 1987a.

Schuckit, M.A.; Gold, E.; and Risch, C. Plasma cortisol levels following ethanol in sons of alcoholics and controls. *Archives of General Psychiatry* 44:942–945, 1987b.

Schuckit, M.A.; Risch, S.C.; and Gold, E.O. Ethanol consumption, ACTH level, and family history of alcoholism. *American Journal of Psychiatry* 145:1391–1395, 1988.

Stockard, C.R., and Papanicolaou, G. A further analysis of the heredity transmission of degeneracy and deformities by the descendants of alcoholized mammals. I. *American Naturalist* 50:68–88, 1916.

Stockard, C.R., and Papanicolaou, G. A further analysis of the heredity transmission of degeneracy and deformities by the descendants of alcoholized
mammals. II. *American Naturalist* 144–177, 1918a.

Stockard, C.R., and Papanicolaou, G. Further studies on the modification
of the germ-cells in mammals: The effect of alcohol on treated
guineapigs and their descendants. *Journal of Experimental Zoology*
26:119–226, 1918b.

Tartar, R.E.; Jacob, T.; and Bremer, D.L. Specific cognitive impairment in
sons of early onset alcoholics. *Alcoholism: Clinical and Experimental Research*
13:786–789, 1989.

Wozniak, D.F.; Cicero, T.J.; Kettinger, L.; and Meyer, E.R. Paternal alcohol
consumption in the rat impairs spatial learning performance in male
offspring. *Psychopharmacology* 105:289–302, 1991.

Yazigi, R.A.; Odem, R.R,; and Polakoski Demonstration of specific binding
of cocaine to human spermatogenesis. *Journal of the American Medical
Association* 266:1956–1959, 1991.

5

The Physical Self

Birth Weight and Handedness in Boys and Girls

E. Petridou, V. Flytzani, S. Youroukos, I.M. Lee, Y.Y. Yen, D. Tong, and D. Trichopoulos

The association between selected demographic variables and birth weight on the one hand and a composite hand preference score based on seven hand tasks (each performed twice) on the other was investigated in a sample of 1387 male and female schoolchildren aged 5 to 10 years old. In multiple regression models left-handedness was significantly more common among boys and among children of better educated mothers and tended to decrease with age. No association was found with respect to urban or rural residence or birth order. Increased birth weight was associated with right-handedness in boys but with left-handedness in girls, and the birth weight by sex interaction term was statistically significant ($p = 0.037$). The demographic associations in the present study are compatible with those reported previously. The different associations of birth weight with hand preference in boys and girls indicate that the prenatal hormonal factors that affect brain lateralization and handedness are qualitatively or quantitatively different in the two sexes and may be differentially associated with birth weight.

The physiology and possible pathophysiology of brain lateralization and handedness have been intensively discussed in the neurodevelopmental and neuropsychological literature (Bryden 1982; Bradshaw and Nettleton 1983; Geschwind and Galaburda 1985; Searleman et al. 1989; Bock and Marsh

Human Biology, Dec 1994, v66 n6 p1093(9).

1991). Although cerebral lateralization and anatomical brain asymmetry (which are likely to be the critical biological variables) do not have a simple obvious relationship with handedness (Geschwind and Galaburda 1985; Le May 1992), handedness is easier to assess and has been investigated more frequently.

Several theories concerning the development of hand preference have been offered, and most focus on the intrauterine environment, invoking either hormonal influences (Geschwind and Galaburda 1985) or focal lesions, possibly associated with perinatal stress (Searleman et al. 1989). The prevailing view is that left-handedness has a familial element, is susceptible to social conditioning, and depends in a critical way on the endocrine environment during pregnancy, notably on testosterone levels in conjunction with availability of testosterone receptors but possibly on estrogen and progesterone levels as well (Bradshaw and Nettleton 1983; Geschwind and Galaburda 1985; Bock and Marsh 1991).

Recently, it was reported that breast cancer may be associated with reversed cerebral asymmetry and hand preference (Olsson and Ingvar 1991; Sandson et al. 1992; Hsieh et al. 1992). Independently, other researchers have suggested that increased levels of estrogens in pregnancy (Trichopoulos 1990), which are associated with higher birth weight (Gerhard et al. 1987; Petridou et al. 1990; Ekbom et al. 1992), may increase the risk of breast cancer in the offspring (Trichopoulos 1990). Although these hypotheses are not widely accepted and although they are not necessarily interrelated, we thought that it would be appropriate to examine whether birth weight is associated with handedness. Because the intra-uterine hormonal environment (notably testosterone levels) varies with the sex of the embryo, interactive effects of birth weight by sex should be assessed. Furthermore, because hand preference reflects an underlying continuous variable (Hardyck and Petrinovich 1977; Geschwind and Galaburda 1985) rather than a sharp "right versus left" contrast, we used a modification of the battery of tests employed by Harris (1958) for the quantitative assessment of hand preference.

MATERIALS AND METHODS

The data were collected over a period of 6 months in 1992 by 8 trained health professionals (visiting nurses), who interviewed and administered the test to all children attending the preschool year and the first 4 grades in 10 schools in Athens and 3 schools in rural areas of Kerkyra, Kalambaca, and Krya Vryssi in Greece. Cooperating teachers in the participating schools asked the parents of the pupils to fill out a simple questionnaire and to provide the children with their health booklet, in which birth weight is recorded by the obstetrician or midwife at the time of birth. Only children who were born after a full-term singleton pregnancy and who had brought their health booklet along with the completed questionnaire were included in the study. Satisfactory information was available for 1387 children, out of a total of about 1500. The demographic

Table 1. Demographic Characteristics of 1387 Children in the Study Group

Variable	N	%
Sex		
Male	726	52.3
Female	661	47.7
Age (yr)		
5	112	8.1
6	135	9.7
7	289	20.8
8	278	20.0
9	270	19.5
10	303	21.9
Residence		
Urban	909	65.5
Rural	478	34.5
Maternal schooling (yr)		
≤ 6	364	26.2
7–11	136	9.8
12	453	32.7
13+	434	31.3
Birth order		
1	689	49.7
2	581	41.9
3+	117	8.4

Table 2. Frequency Distribution of 1387 Children by Recorded Birth Weight

Birth Weight (g)	N	%
≤ 2490	24	1.7
2500–2990	209	15.1
3000–3490	604	43.5
3500–3990	428	30.9
4000–4490	102	7.4
4500+	20	1.4

characteristics of these children and their distribution by recorded birth weight are shown in Tables 1 and 2.

During a 15-minute session, each child was asked to perform the following tasks twice: throw a ball using one hand, write his or her name, draw a picture, cut a piece of paper with provided scissors, use a key to unlock a door, and

Table 3. Distribution of 1387 Children by Lateral Preference in a Series of Seven Hand Tasks

Hand Task	Hand Preference	N	%
Ball throwing	Right	1217	87.7
	Either	59	4.3
	Left	111	8.0
Writing	Right	1259	90.8
	Either	4	0.3
	Left	124	8.9
Drawing	Right	1260	90.8
	Either	4	0.3
	Left	123	8.9
Tooth brushing	Right	1249	90.1
	Either	24	1.8
	Left	114	8.1
Scissors use	Right	1282	92.4
	Either	13	0.9
	Left	92	6.7
Key use	Right	1077	77.7
	Either	195	14.1
	Left	115	8.2
Card dealing	Right	1039	74.9
	Either	67	4.8
	Left	281	20.3

deal a provided pack of cards. The children were also asked to imitate twice how they brush their teeth.

When the child used in both instances the right hand for a particular task, she or he was considered right-handed and was assigned a value of 1 for the respective task; when the particular test was performed twice with the left hand, the child was considered left-handed and was assigned a value of 0 for this task; and when the child used different hands during the two trials of the same task, the child was considered ambidextrous for this task and was assigned a value of 0.5.

A composite score of hand dexterity was generated by adding the seven task–specific values. Thus a child who consistently used his or her right hand throughout was assigned a value of 7, whereas a child who consistently used his or her left hand in all seven tasks was assigned a value of 0.

Statistical analysis was done by multiple regression using the composite hand dexterity score as the dependent variable and demographic characteristics and birth weight as the independent (predictor) variables. The data were analyzed separately for boys and for girls and for the two sexes combined with a sex by birth weight interaction term in the model (Snedecor and Cochran 1967).

RESULTS

Table 3 shows the distribution of the studied children by hand preference in the series of seven tasks, and Table 4 shows the distribution of these children by the composite hand preference score based on the results of all seven hand tasks (each performed twice). The distribution in Table 4 indicates that handedness follows a continuous J-shaped distribution.

The results of the multivariate analyses are presented in Table 5. (Table 5 can be found within the online version of this article, at http://www.infotrac-college.com.) Boys are on the average significantly (p = 0.017) more left-handed, whereas right-handedness increases with age among both boys and girls (although the trend is statistically significant only among boys). Place of residence at the time of the examination (urban versus rural) and birth order (first versus nonfirst) do not show statistically significant, substantial, or consistent associations with handedness. Children of more educated parents tend to be more left-handed, although the trend is clear and reaches statistical significance only when the two sexes are analyzed together.

The birth weight by sex interaction term is statistically significant in the model that included both boys and girls (p = 0.037). It can be seen in the

Table 4. Distribution of 1387 Children by Composite Hand Preference Score Based on Seven Hand Tasks (a)

Handedness Score	Number	%
7.0 (extreme right handed)	772	55.7
6.5	176	12.7
6.0	219	15.8
5.5	46	3.3
5.0	34	2.5
4.5	11	0.8
4.0	12	0.9
3.5	7	0.5
3.0	17	1.2
2.5	10	0.7
2.0	20	1.4
1.5	14	1.0
1.0	16	1.2
0.5	12	0.9
0 (extreme left-handed)	21	1.5

a. Hand tasks indicated in Table 3. For every hand task a value of 1 is assigned to right-handers, a value of 0.5 to those using either or both hands, and a value of 0 to left-handers.

models that contain only boys or only girls that the significant interaction reflects the existence of associations of different direction between birth weight and handedness in the two sexes. Although the two sex-specific associations are not themselves significant, their algebraic difference is sufficiently large to generate a statistically significant interaction term.

DISCUSSION

The ontogeny of cerebral lateralization is poorly understood, but the intrauterine environment, in particular testosterone and estrogen levels in conjunction with their receptors in the brain, apparently is an important determinant (Geschwind and Galaburda 1985; Bock and Marsh 1991). It is also likely that a strong genetic component and postnatal factors, including societal pressures, exercise powerful modifying influences on several expressions of cerebral lateralization (Bradshaw and Nettleton 1983; Geschwind and Galaburda 1985).

The human brain has a consistent pattern of structural asymmetries that appear to be related to handedness in a complex and poorly understood way (Geschwind and Galaburda 1985; Le May 1992). Reports stating that women with breast cancer have a reversed pattern of cerebral asymmetry significantly more frequently than other women (Sandson et al. 1992), that breast cancer appears to be more common in the left breast (Howard et al. 1982; Hsieh and Trichopoulos 1991), that increased birth weight may be a risk factor for breast cancer in the offspring (Ekbom et al. 1992), and that breast cancer could be less common in left-handed women (Olsson and Ingvar 1991; Hsieh et al. 1992) led us to investigate whether birth weight is associated with handedness. Both testosterone and estrogens during pregnancy have been implicated in cerebral lateralization (Geschwind and Galaburda 1985; Bock and Marsh 1991), and these hormones frequently have opposite effects. Accordingly, we have undertaken this study in a population sample of school-age children of both sexes, born after full-term singleton pregnancies, with a view to possible sex interaction.

It is now accepted that cerebral lateralization and its various functional expressions represent continuous variables and not categorical contrasts (Annett 1970). Several tests have been developed to assess handedness quantitatively (Harris 1958; Oldfield 1971; Provins et al. 1982). In the present study a battery of widely used tests (Harris 1958) has been adapted to the Greek conditions and limitations and has been used by trained health professionals.

The study sample was not strictly representative of Greek school-children, but this should not affect the validity of the results, because selection was based on demographic criteria and logistical realities, and it was clearly independent of the outcome variable (handedness). Furthermore, the identified significant associations of right-handedness with age (positive), male sex (negative), and maternal educational status (negative) are compatible with those reported in the literature and indicate that the study was essentially valid and sufficiently powerful (Oldfield 1971; Bradshaw and Nettleton 1983). Last, no relation was noted in the present study between birth order and handedness, in agreement with the collective evidence in the literature (Nachshon and Denno 1986; Schwartz 1988; Searleman et al. 1989).

No association between birth weight and hand preference was evident in the National Institutes of Health Collaborative Perinatal Project (Ehrlichman et al. 1982) but, as that study indicates, hand preference was assessed in a simple way that did not allow quantification of handedness. Several investigations have explored pathological perinatal conditions in relation to handedness (McManus 1981; Ashton 1982; Schwartz 1988), but we are not aware of other studies that have examined the association between the normal range of birth weight of children born after full-term singleton pregnancies and a quantitative estimator of their handedness.

In this study right-handedness was associated positively with birth weight in boys and negatively in girls. These associations were not themselves statistically significant, but the trends were opposite and the difference between the two slopes (regression coefficients) was statistically significant. Estrogens in pregnancy are known growth factors and are positively associated with birth weight (Gerhard et al. 1987; Petridou et al. 1990; Ekbom et al. 1992). Furthermore, both estrogens and testosterone present during pregnancy have been implicated in cerebral lateralization (Geschwind and Galaburda 1985; Bock and Marsh 1991), and the presence of higher levels of testosterone in male embryos provides some biologic plausibility to the existence of an interaction between birth weight and sex in the eventual determination of hand preference.

Cerebral lateralization is likely to be a complicated process, and the development of handedness is clearly multifactorial. Moreover, the association of breast cancer with cerebral asymmetry, handedness, and birth weight are at present tenuous. A sex-dependent relation of birth weight with handedness, if confirmed by other investigators, could provide an insight into the complex interrelations between intrauterine hormonal environment, cerebral lateralization, and, perhaps, the origins of breast cancer.

CRITICAL THINKING QUESTIONS

1. One of the findings of the Petridou et al. study was that right-handedness tended to increase with age. Why might this be the case?

2. Higher levels of estrogen during pregnancy are associated with higher birth weight. In the current study, Petridou et al. found that males and females showed differential effects of birth weight on left-handedness, with females showing a positive relationship and males showing a negative relationship. Explain why differences in the prenatal levels of estrogens might help explain this gender difference.

LITERATURE CITED

Annett, M. 1970. A classification of hand preference by association analysis. *Br. J. Psychol.* 61:303–321.

Ashton, G.C. 1982. Handedness: An alternative hypothesis. *Behav. Genet.* 12:125–147.

Bock, G.R., and J. Marsh, eds. 1991. Biological Asymmetry and Handedness. CIBA Foundation Symposium 162. New York: Wiley.

Bradshaw, J.L., and N.C. Nettleton. 1983. *Human Cerebral Asymmetry.* Englewood Cliffs, NJ: Prentice-Hall.

Bryden, M.P. 1982. *Laterality: Functional Asymmetry in the Intact Brain.* New York: Academic Press.

Ehrlichman, H., P. Zoccolotti, and D. Owen. 1982. Perinatal factors in hand and eye preference: Data from the collaborative perinatal project. *Int. J. Neurosci.* 17: 17–22.

Ekbom, A., D. Trichopoulos, H.-O. Adami et al. 1992. Evidence of prenatal influences on breast cancer risk. *Lancet* 340:1015–1018.

Gerhard, I., B. Vollmar, B. Runnebaum et al. 1987. Weight percentile at birth. II. Prediction by endocrinological and sonographic measurements. *Eur. J. Obstet. Gynecol. Reprod. Biol.* 26:313–328.

Geschwind, N., and A.M. Galaburda. 1985. Cerebral lateralization: Biological mechanisms, associations, and pathology. I. A hypothesis and a program for research. *Arch. Neurol.* 42:428–459.

Hardyck, C., and L.F. Petrinovich. 1977. Left-handedness. *Psychol. Bull.* 84:385–404.

Harris, A.J. 1958. *The Harris Test of Lateral Dominance: Manual of Directions.* New York: Psychological Corp.

Howard, J., N.L. Petrakis, I.D. Bross et al. 1982. Handedness and breast cancer laterality: Testing a hypothesis. *Hum. Biol.* 54:365–371.

Hsieh, C.-C., and D. Trichopoulos. 1991. Breast size, handedness, and breast cancer risk. *Eur. J. Cancer* 27:131–135.

Hsieh, C.-C., A. Ekbom, and D. Trichopoulos. 1992. Left handedness and breast cancer risk. *Eur. J. Cancer* 29:167.

Le May, M. 1992. Left-right dissymmetry, handedness. *Am. J. Neuroradiol.* 13:493–504.

McManus, I.C. 1981. Handedness and birth stress. *Psychol. Med.* 11:485–496.

Nachshon, I., and D. Denno. 1986. Birth order and lateral preferences. *Cortex* 22:567–578.

Oldfield, R.C. 1971. The assessment and analysis of handedness: The Edinburgh Inventory. *Neuropsychologia* 9:97–113.

Olsson, H., and C. Ingvar. 1991. Left-handedness is uncommon in breast cancer patients. *Eur. J. Cancer* 27: 1694–1695.

Petridou, E., K. Panagiotopoulou, K. Katsouyanni et al. 1990. Tobacco smoking, pregnancy estrogens, and birth weight. *Epidemiology* 1:247–250.

Provins, K.A., A.D. Milner, and P. Kerr. 1982. Asymmetry of mammal preference and performance. *Percept. Mot. Skills* 54:179–194.

Sandson, T.A., P.Y. Wen, and M. Le May. 1992. Reversed cerebral asymmetry in women with breast cancer. *Lancet* 339:523–524.

Schwartz, M. 1988. Handedness, prenatal stress, and pregnancy complications. *Neuropsychologia* 26:925–929.

Searleman, A., C. Porac, and S. Coren. 1989. Relationship between birth order, birth stress, and lateral preferences: A critical review. *Psychol. Bull.* 3:397–408.

Snedecor, G.W., and W.G. Cochran. 1967. *Statistical Methods.* Ames, IA: Iowa State University Press.

Trichopoulos, D. 1990. Hypothesis: Does breast cancer originate in utero? *Lancet* 335:939–940.

6

Perception

Flavor Programming During Infancy

Julie A. Mennella, Cara E. Griffin, and Gary K. Beauchamp

Objective. *Although individuals differ substantially in their flavor and food preferences, the source of such differences remains a mystery. The present experimental study was motivated by clinical observations that early experience with formulas establishes subsequent preferences.*

Design. *Infants whose parents had chosen to formula-feed them were randomized into 1 of 4 groups by the second week of life. One group was assigned to be fed a milk-based formula (Enfamil), whereas another was assigned to be fed (Nutramigen), a particularly unpleasant-tasting protein hydrolysate formula. The remaining groups were assigned to be fed Nutramigen for 3 months and Enfamil for 4 months; the timing of exposure differed between the groups, After 7 months of exposure, infants were videotaped on 3 separate days while feeding, in counterbalanced order, Enfamil, Nutramigen, and Alimentum, a novel hydrolysate formula.*

Results. *For each of the 4 interrelated measures of behavior (intake, duration of formula feeding, facial expressions, and mothers' judgments of infant acceptance), previous exposure to Nutramigen significantly enhanced subsequent acceptance of both Nutramigen and Alimentum. Seven months of exposure led to greater acceptance than did 3 months.*

Conclusions. *The bases for clinical difficulties in introducing hydrolysate formulas during older infancy are clarified in this study. More broadly, variation in formula flavor*

Reproduced with permission from Pediatrics, Vol. 113, Page(s) 840–845, Copyright
© 2004 by the AAP.

provided a useful model for demonstrating experimentally the effects of long-term exposure differences on later acceptance. Such early variation, under more species-typical circumstances (eg, via exposure to different flavors in amniotic fluid and mothers' milk), may underlie individual differences in food acceptability throughout the life span.

S ources of individual differences in food preferences and habits are one of the most fundamental mysteries of human behavior. Although genetic differences may underlie some of these differences, (1, 2) for omnivores such as humans, it is important that there not be too many genetically determined restrictions on what constitutes an acceptable food. (3) Instead, as suggested by a growing body of data from other sensory and motor systems, (4–6) experience may have important influences on later functioning and preferences. We hypothesized that there are sensitive periods during which the human infant is particularly likely to form flavor preferences and aversions that, in turn, serve as the foundation for lifelong food habits. (7)

Recently, we suggested that a particularly apt model system to explore potential early sensitive periods in flavor learning involves the inherent flavor variations characteristic of infant formulas and the ontogenic changes in acceptance/rejection of particular flavors. (7–9) Within each of the 3 classes of commercially available formulas (ie, cow's milk based, soy protein based, and hydrolyzed protein based), and in particular between the hydrolysate- and milk-based varieties, differences in sensory quality (flavor) are profound. Milk-based formulas are often described as having low levels of sweetness and being "sour and cereal-like," whereas hydrolyzed protein-based formulas are of a most unpleasant character, with a bitter and sour taste profile, unpleasant odor volatiles, and a horrible after taste. (10, 11) The extreme unpalatability of hydrolysates, which supply protein nutrients in a "predigested" form, is likely caused by both its processing and composition, because many amino acids and small peptides taste sour and bitter and are characterized by unpleasant volatile components. (12)

There are striking developmental changes in infants' acceptance of hydrolysate formulas. Infants ~4 months old readily accept these formulas on first exposure, whereas older infants strongly reject them within the first few minutes of feeding. (8, 9, 13) Clinicians report that infants who consume a hydrolysate formula from early infancy readily continue to accept it well after 5 months of age. (7) These observations suggest that there is a profound change at ~4 months of age in the infants' perception of these formulas and that early experience modifies later acceptance.

To test rigorously the suggestion derived from such cross-sectional data, we designed a longitudinal experimental study wherein infants were assigned randomly to different experience groups. This permitted precise control of exposure history and consequently is the ideal test of the hypothesis that prior exposure to a particular flavored formula impacts later acceptance of that and other formulas. More generally, this experimental study can provide a convenient and powerful model system for investigating the existence of sensitive periods in the development of human flavor preferences.

METHODS

Subjects

Mothers who had chosen previously to formula feed their term newborns were recruited by advertisements in local newspapers. When the infant was <3 weeks old and the mother's decision not to lactate was well established, the mother–infant pairs (24% African American and 76% white) were randomized into 1 of 4 groups (Table 1) differing in the timing and type of formula (ie, Enfamil: milk-based formula [E]; Nutramigen: protein hydrolysate formula [N]) that the infant was fed during each month of the 7-month study. One group, EEEEEEE (here-after referred to as the control group; n = 14), was assigned to a milk-based formula, Enfamil, whereas another group, NNNNNNN (n = 12), was assigned to the protein hydrolysate formula Nutramigen during the entire 7-month period of the study. The 2 other groups, NNNEEEE (n = 15) and EENNNEE (n = 12), were assigned to feed Nutramigen for specified periods during their first 7 months of life, as indicated by the Ns and Es in the groups' names. Infants were fed on demand and ad libitum. All procedures used in this study were approved by the Office of Regulatory Affairs at the University of Pennsylvania, and informed consent was obtained before entry into the study. Mothers were compensated for their participation in the study.

Monthly Procedures

At the start of the study and then again at the beginning of each 1-month cycle, mothers came to the Monell Center (Philadelphia, PA), where they

Table 1. Description of Experimental Groups

	Experimental Groups			
Infant Age at Start of Exposure, mo*	**EEEEEEE**	**NNNEEEE**	**EENNNEE**	**NNNNNNN**
0.5	Enfamil	Nutramigen	Enfamil	Nutramigen
1.5	Enfamil	Nutramigen	Enfamil	Nutramigen
2.5	Enfamil	Nutramigen	Nutramigen	Nutramigen
3.5	Enfamil	Enfarnil	Nutramigen	Nutramigen
4.5	Enfamil	Enfamil	Nutramigen	Nutramigen
5.5	Enfamil	Enfamil	Enfamil	Nutramigen
6.5	Enfamil	Enfamil	Enfamil	Nutramigen

*Infants' age at the start of each 4-week exposure period (±1 week). Each infant was evaluated at the end of each month and at the end of the study at 7.5 months. The names of the groups refer to the month of life that infants were fed Nutramigen or Enfamil.

were videotaped feeding their infants the formula consumed since the last visit. The infants' weights and heights before feeding and the amount of formula consumed during this midday feed were recorded. These monthly evaluations were performed to ensure compliance with the study protocols, to chart infants' acceptance of the assigned formulas, and to obtain accurate information on the introduction of cereal, fruits, and vegetables. The next month's supply of formula (with the labels removed) then was distributed. Mothers were informed that the formula was either Enfamil or Nutramigen. Mothers completed questionnaires to evaluate their food and general neophobia at the end of the first and last monthly visit (14) as well as questionnaires related to infant temperament at 0.5, 3.5, and 7.5 months. (15, 16)

Test Procedures at the End of the 7-Month Exposure Period

By using methodologies established in our laboratory, (8, 9) infants were tested on 3 separate days within 1 week. At the same time of day and 4.1 ± 0.2 hours after their last formula feed, each infant was videotaped feeding the hydrolysate formula Nutramigen on 1 test day, the milk-based formula Enfamil on another day, and Alimentum (a novel hydrolysate formula to all infants) on yet another test day. Testing occurred under naturalistic conditions in which the infants determined the pacing and duration of feeding. The order of testing was counterbalanced between and within groups, and the mothers were not aware of the hypothesis or which formula was being fed to the infant during each of the 3 test sessions. The mothers refrained from talking or making faces during the feeding sessions to eliminate any potential influence of the mother's verbal or facial responses on her infant's behaviors (17); replays of the videotapes verified that this indeed was the case. Mothers were instructed to feed the infants at their customary pace until the infant refused the bottle 3 consecutive times, using the criterion that the infant exhibited such behaviors as turning his or her head away, pushing the bottle away, crying, or becoming playful. The experimenter, who was unaware of the hypothesis of the study, sat behind the video camera, which was placed at the far corner of the testing room ~10 to 12 feet from the mother-infant dyad, and was out of view of the mother and her infant. Immediately after each feeding session, the mothers then rated how much they thought their infant liked the formula on a 9-point scale. (8, 9) Intermediate ratings were to be marked at the appropriate locations between the extremes such that ratings could range from 1 (did not like at all) to 9 (liked very much).

Trained raters who were unaware of the experimental conditions and hypothesis of the studies scored the videotaped records to determine the length of the formula feed and frequency of various facial expressions. During scoring, the sound was turned off so that the raters would not be influenced by the infants' vocalizations. The Ekman and Friesen Facial Action Coding System, (18) an anatomically based system that specifies facial movements in terms of minimally distinguishable actions of the facial muscles (termed action unit), was used to code a variety of facial expressions. Based on previous research of the type of facial responses made by human infants and other primates to a variety of taste and olfactory stimuli that differed in hedonic valence, (19–21) we determined the frequency of 4 negative facial expressions (ie, nose wrinkling, frowning, upper-lip raise, and gaping). Two observers individually scored the videotapes of 41 feedings selected at random. Reliability for scoring of each of the facial responses and the length of the feeding was >85% (P < .0001).

Statistical Analyses

For each infant, we determined the total intake (milliliters) and length (minutes) of each feed, the frequency of negative facial expressions during the first 2 minutes of feeding, and mothers' ratings of their infants' enjoyment of the formulas during each of the 3 test sessions conducted at the end of the 7-month exposure period. To determine whether there were significant differences among the 4 groups, we conducted separate repeated-measures analyses of variance (ANOVA) with group (n = 4) as the grouping factor and type of formula (n = 3) as the within-subjects factor. Significant effects in the ANOVA were probed by Tukey honest significant difference tests to determine whether the 3 exposure groups differed from each other as well as the control group. All summary statistics are expressed as mean ± standard error, and the level of significance was P < .05 for the ANOVA and P < .02 for the Tukey tests.

RESULTS

Subject Characteristics

There were no significant differences among the 4 groups in the ages of mothers and infants, the number of females/males, or the infants' weights and lengths at the start of the study. There also were no significant group differences for any of the various measures of infant temperament, the age at which infants were introduced to solid foods, or maternal measures of food and general neophobia (all P values > .10).

Infants' Formula Acceptance Throughout
the 7-Month Study

There were no significant differences between the groups in the infants' acceptance of the formula that they were fed during the previous month throughout the 7-month study (F[3,49 df] = 0.91; P = .44; data not shown), thus indicating compliance with study procedures.

Infants' Acceptance of Hydrolysate Formulas
at 7.5 Months of Age

There was a significant interaction between groups and the infants' acceptance of the 3 brands of formulas when tested at the end of the 7-month exposure period (intake: F[6,98 df] = 8.12 and $P < .000000$; duration of feed: F[6,98 df] = 5.60 and $P < .00005$). The 3 groups of Nutramigen-exposed infants drank significantly more and spent more time feeding Nutramigen and Alimentum when compared with those infants who were fed only Enfamil during the first 7 months of life (Table 2 and Fig 1 [Figure Omitted]; all P values $< .05$).

Table 2. Infants' Feeding Behaviors and Mothers' Perceptions After the 7-Month Exposure Period

	Experimental Group	
	EEEEEEE	NNNEEEE
Intake, ml		
Enfamil	160.9 ± 22.3	237.1 ± 21.6*
Nutramigen	22.7 ± 21.7	88.9 ± 21.0*†
Alimentum	43.9 ± 21.2	120.7 ± 20.4*
Duration of feed, min		
Enfamil	7.2 ± 1.3	12.0 ± 1.2*
Nutramigen	1.8 ± 1.2	6.2 ± 1.1*†
Alimentum	3.1 ± 1.5	8.1 ± 1.5*
Frequency of negative facial action units during first 2 min of feed		
Enfamil	3.9 ± 1.8	1.5 ± 11.8
Nutramigen	9.5 ± 1.5	4.5 ± 1.4*
Alimentum	5.7 ± 1.3	3.3 ± 1.2
Mothers' ratings of infants' acceptance of formula: (range: 1–9; 1 = did not enjoy at all)		
Enfamil	7.7 ± 0.6	8.5 ± 0.6
Nutramigen	1.4 ± 0.7	4.6 ± 0.6*†
Alimentum	2.6 ± 0.8	4.2 ± 0.8
No. of subjects (females/males):	14(7:7)	15 (6:9)
Intake, ml		
Enfamil	158.8 ± 24.1	119.1 ± 22.9
Nutramigen	92.6 ± 23.4*†	194.3 ± 23.4*
Alimentum	145.5 ± 22.9*	119.3 ± 24.1*

(*continued*)

Table 2. (continued)

	Experimental Group	
	EENNNEE	**NNNNNNN**
Duration of feed, min		
Enfamil	7.3 ± 1.4	7.1 ± 1.4
Nutramigen	6.0 ± 1.3*†	11.8 ± 1.3*
Alimentum	8.4 ± 1.6*	8.1 ± 1.6*
Frequency of negative facial action units during first 2 min of feed		
Enfamil	3.8 ± 2.0	6.4 ± 2.0
Nutramigen	4.8 ± 1.6*	1.1 ± 1.6*
Alimentum	4.3 ± 1.4	4.2 ± 1.4
Mothers' ratings of infants' acceptance of formula: (range: 1–9; 1 = did not enjoy at all)		
Enfamil	7.3 ± 0.7	4.9 ± 0.7*
Nutramigen	4.6 ± 0.7*†	8.3 ± 0.7*
Alimentum	5.3 ± 0.9	6.1 ± 0.9*
No. of subjects (females/males):	12 (8:4)	12 (5:7)

The amount of formula consumed, the duration of the feeding, the frequency of negative and positive facial action units displayed, and the mothers' ratings of their infants' acceptance of formula are shown for each of the 3 testing sessions in which 7.5-month-old infants consumed, in counterbalanced order, Enfamil, Nutramigen, and Alimentum.

The groups differed in the type of formula consumed during the first 7 months of life. Group EEEEEEE was assigned to be fed Enfamil and group NNNNNNN was assigned to be fed the protein hydrolysate formula Nutramigen during the entire 7-month period of the study. Groups NNNEEEE and EENNNEE were assigned to feed Nutramigen for 3 months and Enfamil for 4 months; the timing of exposure differed between the groups. The values shown are means ± standard error.

*$P < 0.05$ for the comparison with the EEEEEEE group.

(†) $P < 0.0.5$ for the comparison of group NNNEEEE or EENNNEE with the NNNNNNN group.

(All figures referenced can be found within the online version of this article, at http://www.infotrac-college.com.) However, exposure to Nutramigen for 7 months (group NNNNNNN) resulted in greater acceptance of the Nutramigen when compared with exposure for 3 months (groups NNNEEEE and EENNNEE).

There was also a significant effect of group on the number of negative facial actions displayed while feeding the formulas (F[6,98 df] = 2.51; $P < .05$). Infants in groups NNNNNNN, NNNEEEE, and EENNNEE made significantly less negative facial responses while ingesting Nutramigen when compared with infants exposed only to the milk-based Enfamil formula

(Fig 1) [Figure Omitted]. Differences in facial responses made while feeding Nutramigen are also illustrated in Fig 2 [Figure Omitted].

Mothers' Perceptions

There was a significant group-by-formula interaction (F[6,96 df] = 9.96; $P = .00000$) in mothers' perceptions of their infants' behaviors that was consistent with the infants' acceptance patterns (Table 2). Mothers of infants in the 3 groups who had previous exposure to Nutramigen were significantly more likely to report that their infant enjoyed feeding Nutramigen when compared with the infants who had never been exposed to Nutramigen. In addition, mothers of infants who were exposed only to Nutramigen during the first 7 months of life were significantly more likely to report that their infants liked feeding Alimentum but disliked feeding Enfamil when compared with the group never exposed to Nutramigen (P < .0001).

DISCUSSION

Previous exposure to a hydrolysate formula, Nutramigen, enhanced its later acceptance. Infants who were never fed Nutramigen during the first 7 months of life strongly rejected it when it was first offered at 7.5 months, whereas those who were regularly fed this formula during most of their infancy responded to it as if it were very acceptable at 7.5 months of age. Between these 2 extremes, infants fed Nutramigen either during their first 3 months of life or during months 3 through 5 were generally more accepting than those who had never been fed this formula but less so than those fed Nutramigen for the entire 7 months. No differences were evident between these 2 midexposure groups, providing no evidence for differential potency of exposure during different portions of early infancy.

Sensory Basis for Differential Responsiveness

The remarkable consistency among the 3 indices of acceptance (Fig 1) [Figure Omitted] suggests that these measures reflect a common underlying factor that is most likely differential responses to the formulas based on their chemosensory attributes. Strengthening this conclusion are the data on expressive responses (mothers' judgments and analyses of facial expressions) that most likely directly reveal hedonic responses to sensory stimuli. Based on adult sensory profiling of these formulas, the 2 primary sensory pathways involved are likely taste and olfaction. (7)

Concerning taste, hydrolysate formulas taste more bitter and sour than most traditional milk-based formulas including Enfamil. Thus, it would not be surprising that hydrolysate formulas would be rejected more strongly, because newborns reject bitter and very sour stimuli. (20–23) What makes this hypothesis questionable is that rejection does not occur until after 4 months of age. However, at least as it concerns bitterness perception, there are multiple classes of bitter compounds presumably recognized by members of a large family of bitter receptors. (24) The bitterness of hydrolysate formulas, probably caused by bitterness of free amino acids and small peptides (12) and possibly other substances produced during processing, may be detected by receptors that do not mature until the infant is several months old.

Concerning olfaction, that the cloying, unpleasant, nauseating flavor and aftertaste of hydrolysates can be reduced substantially if the olfactory component is eliminated by tasting hydrolysates with the nares held closed, implicates olfaction in the adults' and perhaps the infants' hedonic judgments, it has been suggested that although hedonic judgments for tastes are relatively "hard wired" or determined innately, (25) hedonic responses to the olfactory components of flavor are influenced strongly by experience. (26) Thus, the observed changes in response to the hydrolysate formulas with age and prior experience may depend on developmental and experiential changes ("olfactory imprinting") (27, 28) in response to the volatile components of the formulas.

Persistence

There are indications that the effects of early experience to hydrolysate formulas may be long lived. In a prior study, we found that 4- to 5-year-old children who were fed hydrolysates during their infancy exhibited more positive responses to sensory attributes associated with them (eg, sour taste and aroma) several years after their last exposure to the formula when compared with same-aged children without such experience. (26, 29) In addition, clinical studies on adolescent children with phenylketonuria who went off their modified hydrolysate formula suggest that they can often, albeit with some difficulty, return to formulas on which they were reared as infants. (30–32) Because these formulas are unpalatable to adolescents who have not had infant exposure, this relative ease of return could reflect the long-term effects of prior experience. (33)

Generality

The effects observed in these studies are likely of substantially broad significance, revealing a fundamental feature of mammalian dietary learning. Studies of humans and other animals have shown that fetuses are bathed in flavored amniotic fluids that reflect in part the pregnant animals' diet. (34) After birth, mammals are exposed further to milk that is flavored by the diet the nursing mother is consuming. Consequently, even during very early development, mammals usually sample a large and varied set of flavor compounds. We suggest that these "natural" experiences with flavored amniotic fluid and milk serve to familiarize the young infant with flavors of the dietary constituents the mother consumes and establish them as acceptable and preferred. (35) Culturally determined flavor preferences, one of the most enduring characteristics of an ethnic group, (36, 37) can be understood in the context of early lavor exposure. Flavors common to an ethnic group are experienced early in life, at a time when the pregnant or lactating mother is most likely being fed foods most characteristic of and most revered by that particular culture. (37)

Clinical Implications

Some of the original impetus for this work came from questions raised by clinicians concerning the practical difficulties in introducing hydrolysate formulas to older infants as well as the long-term effects of early feeding. (38) Our studies reveal the basis for these clinical impressions and suggest some remedies.

First, if infants are to be placed on hydrolysate formulas, they should be introduced as early as possible and certainly before 4 months of age. A strategy of gradually introducing hydrolysates to older infants by mixing it with regular, milk-based formula at increasing proportions seems reasonable (39) but to our knowledge has not been experimentally tested.

Second, caregivers who feed infants recognize hydrolysates are very unpalatable. They may feel that they are punishing their child by feeding such an offensively flavored formula. Our studies make it clear that this is not the case if infants are started early, however. The infant will not only accept it readily but will find it palatable.

Third, there is room to develop more palatable hydrolysate formulas. The first step in such a program should be to determine the specific sensory aspects of these formulas that are offensive to the naive infant and preferred by the exposed infant. Such information would help suggest a rational strategy for favorably modifying current formulations.

CONCLUSIONS

These data underscore one of the most fundamental differences in the experiences of the formula- and breastfed infants. To be sure, the nutrient composition of formula is held to standards and regulation that are based, in part, on the analyses of human milk. However, unlike breast milk, the flavors of all types of formulas are monotonous and lack sensory information on the dietary choices of the mother. Thus, the formula-fed infant is being deprived of rich and varied sensory experiences that at one time were common to all mammalian young. How this impacts on later food habits and flavor preferences remains to be determined, but it seems likely that the consequences could be profound.

Julie A. Mennella, PhD; Cara E. Griffin, BS; and Gary K. Beauchamp, PhD
From the Monell Chemical Senses Center, Philadelphia, Pennsylvania
   Received for publication May 5, 2003; accepted Sep 29, 2003.
   Address correspondence to Julie A. Mennella, PhD, 3500 Market St, Philadelphia,
PA 19104-3308. E-mail: mennella@monell.org

ABBREVIATIONS. E, Enfamil; N, Nutramigen; ANOVA, analysis of variance.

ACKNOWLEDGMENTS

This research was supported by National Institutes of Health grant HD37119, and the research apprenticeship of Ms Jhamirah Howard was supported by grants from The Annenberg Foundation and Mrs Patricia Kind. We also thank the Nutritional Division of Mead Johnson for supplying the Enfamil and Nutramigen.

We appreciate the expert technical assistance of Ms Jhamirah Howard and Ms Coren Jagnow.

CRITICAL THINKING QUESTIONS

1. In general, young infants are more accepting of novel foods than are older infants. This developmental change in food preferences has been viewed by some psychologists as representing an adaptation such that infants become increasingly wary of strange foods as they become capable of self-propelled movement (i.e., crawling, walking). Speculate on why such an adaptation might be advantageous for infants.

2. Typically, food preferences are viewed as a product of social learning. In other words, we learn from others which foods are disgusting and which are pleasant. In the Menella, Griffin & Beauchamp study, it appears that there is a sensitive period for the development of these preferences during which environmental input profoundly influences later taste preferences. Given that the existence of a sensitive period is often taken as evidence for the biological basis of a characteristic, yet the particular foods that a baby prefers are the result of environmental exposure to those foods, would we say that taste is governed more by biology or environment?

3. In the Menella, Griffin & Beauchamp study, parents of infants in the experimental group were asked to feed their children Nutramigen, a bitter, sour formula that many infants and adults find extremely unpalatable. Discuss the ethical issues involved with giving young infants formula known to be distasteful, and under what conditions it would be appropriate to stop the experiment.

REFERENCES

1. Duffy VB, Bartoshuk LM. Food acceptance and genetic variation in taste. *J Am Diet Assoc.* 2000;100:647–655

2. Drewnowski A, Henderson SA, Barratt-Fornell A. Genetic taste markers and food preferences. *Drug Metab Dispos.* 2001;29:535–538

3. Rozin P. The selection of foods by rats, humans, and other animals. In: Rosenblatt JS, Hind RA, Shaw E, Beer C, eds. *Advances in the Study of Behavior.* Vol 6. New York, NY: Academic Press; 1976:21–76

4. Hurford JR. The evolution of the critical period for language acquisition. *Cognition.* 1991;40:159–201

5. Elston JS, Timms C. Clinical evidence for the onset of the sensitive period in infancy. *Br J Ophthalmol.* 1992;76:327–328

6. Kuhl PK, Williams KA, Lacerda F, Stevens KN, Lindblom B. Linguistic experience alters phonetic perception in infants by six months of age. *Science.* 1992;255:606–608

7. Beauchamp GK, Mennella JA. Sensitive periods in the development of human flavor perception and preference. In: Annales Nestle, Nestle Nutrition Workshop Series. Vol 56. Vevey, Switzerland: Nestec Ltd; 1998: 19–31

8. Mennella JA, Beauchamp GK. Developmental changes in the infants' acceptance of protein–hydrolysate formula and its relation to mothers' eating habits. *J Dev Behav Pediatr.* 1996;17:386–391

9. Mennella JA, Beauchamp GK. Development and bad taste. *Pediatr Asthma Allergy Immunol.* 1998;12:161–163

10. Cook DA, Sarett HP. Design of infant formulas for meeting normal and special need. In: Lifshitz F, ed. *Pediatric Nutrition: infant Feeding, Deficiencies, Disease.* New York, NY: Marcel Dekker, Inc; 1982

11. Lee YH. Food-processing approaches to altering allergenic potential of milk-based formula. *J Pediatr.* 1992;121:S47–S50

12. Schiffman SS, Dackis C. Taste of nutrients: amino acids, vitamins, and fatty acids. *Percept Psychophys.* 1975;17:140–146

13. Mennella JA. Development of the chemical senses and the programming of flavor preference. In: Physiologic/Immunologic Responses to Dietary Nutrients: Role of Elemental and Hydrolysate Formulas in Management of the Pediatric Patient. Report of the 107th Conference on Pediatric Research. Columbus, OH: Ross Products Division, Abbott Laboratories; 1998:201–208

14. Pliner P, Hobden K. Development of a scale to measure the trait of food neophobia in humans. *Appetite.* 1992;19:105–120

15. Medoff-Cooper B, Carey WB, McDevitt SC. The early infancy temperament questionnaire. *J Dev Behav Pediatr.* 1993;14:230–235

16. Carey WB, McDevitt SC. Revision of the Infant Temperament Questionnaire. *Pediatrics.* 1978;61:735–739

17. Meltzoff AN, Moore MK. Imitation of facial and manual gestures by human neonates. *Science.* 1977;198:75–78

18. Ekman P, Friesen W. *The Facial Action Coding System.* Palo Alto, CA: Consulting Psychologists Press; 1978

19. Soussignan R, Schaal B, Marlier L, Jiang T. Facial and autonomic responses to biological and artificial olfactory stimuli in human neonates: re examining early hedonic discrimination of odors. *Physiol Behav.* 1997; 62:745–758

20. Steiner JE, Glaser D, Hawilo ME, Berridge KC. Comparative expression of hedonic impact: affective reactions to taste by human infants and other primates. *Neurosci Biobehav Rev.* 2001;25:53–74

21. Rosenstein D, Oster H. Differential facial responses to four basic tastes in newborns. *Child Dev.* 1988;59:1555–1568

22. Kajuira H, Cowart J, Beauchamp GK. Early developmental changes in bitter taste responses in human infants. *Dev Psychobiol.* 1992;25:375–386

23. Steiner JE. Facial expressions of the neonate infant indicating the hedonics of food related chemical stimuli. In: Weiffenbach JM, ed. *Taste and Development: The Genesis of Sweet Preference.* Washington, DC: US Government Printing Office; 1977

24. Chandrashekar J, Mueller KL, Hoon MA, et al. T2Rs function as bitter taste receptors. *Cell.* 2000;100:703–711

25. Bartoshuk LM, Beauchamp GK. Chemical senses. *Annu Rev Psychol.* 1994;45:419–449

26. Mennella JA, Beauchamp GK. Flavor experiences during formula feeding are related to preferences during childhood. *Early Human Dev.* 2002;68:71–82

27. Woo CC, Leon M. Sensitive period for neural and behavioral response development to learned odors. *Brain Res.* 1987;433:308–313

28. Sullivan RM, Landers M, Yeaman B, Wilson DA. Good memories of bad events in infancy. *Nature.* 2002;407:38–39

29. Liem DG, Mennella JA. Sweet and sour preferences during childhood: role of early experiences. *Dev Psychobiol.* 2002;41:388–395

30. National Institutes of Health Consensus Development Panel. National Institutes of Health Consensus Development Conference statement: phenylketonuria: screening and management, October 16–18, 2000. *Pediatrics.* 2001;108:972–982

31. Schuett VE, Gurda RF, Brown ES. Diet discontinuation policies and practices of PKU clinics in the United States. *Am J Public Health.* 1980; 70:498–503

32. Schuett VE, Brown ES, Michals K. Reinstitution of diet therapy in PKU patients from twenty-two clinics. *Am J Public Health.* 1985;75:39–42

33. Owada M, Aoki K, Kitagawa T. Taste preferences and feeding behaviour in children with phenylketonuria on a semisynthetic diet. *Eur J Pediatr.* 2000;159:846–850

34. Mennella JA, Johnson A, Beauchamp GK. Garlic ingestion by pregnant women alters the odor of amniotic fluid. *Chem Senses.* 1995;20:207–209

35. Mennella JA, Jagnow CJ, Beauchamp GK. Prenatal and postnatal flavor learning by human infants. *Pediatrics.* 2001;107(6). Available at: www.pediatrics.org/cgi/content/full/107/6/e88

36. Rozin P. The acquisition of food habits and preferences. In: Mattarazzo HD, Weiss SM, Herd JA, Miller NE, Weiss SM, eds. Behavioral Health: *A handbook of Health Enhancement and Disease Prevention.* New York, NY: John Wiley and Sons; 1984:590–607

37. Mennella JA. The flavor world of infants: a cross-cultural perspective. *Nutr Today.* 1997;32:142–151

38. Beauchamp GK, Mennella JA. Early feeding and the acquisition of flavor preferences. In: Boulton J, Laron Z, Rey J, eds. *Long-Term Consequences of Early Feeding.* Nestle Nutrition Workshop Series Book 36. Philadelphia, PA: Lippincott-Raven Publishers; 1996:163–177

39. Coping With Colic: Helpful Tips for Parents [audiotape]. Evansville, IN: Mead Johnson; 1990

7

Cognition

Gender Difference in Horizontality Performance Before and After Training

Gowri Parameswaran

To investigate why some individuals, especially females, fail Piaget's horizontality task, the author administered Piaget's horizontality task, the rod and frame field-dependence task, Bem's Sex Role Inventory, and a history of spatial activities questionnaire to 122 undergraduates. Individuals who failed the horizontality task were trained on this task, and after 1 month all participants were administered a horizontality posttest. Hierarchical regression analysis revealed that field dependence was related significantly to both pretest and posttest scores. Sex and masculine sex role concept were related to pretest but not to posttest scores. The implications of these findings for group differences in horizontality performance are discussed.

Piaget and Inhelder (1956) used the horizontality and verticality tasks to test children's attainment of Euclidean reference frames. Subsequent researchers have found that males have performed better on the task than females have (Liben, 1991). This difference was manifested by the age of 7 years and held for adults (Linn & Peterson, 1985).

Journal of Genetic Psychology, March 1995, v156 n1 p105(9).

Several explanations have been offered for gender differences in the performance of the horizontality tasks. Some of these explanations center on biological differences between males and females, and others emphasize the differences in the experiences of males and females.

Biological explanations emphasize (a) genetic differences between males and females (Thomas & Jamison, 1981a, 1981b), (b) differences in the rate of maturation between males and females (males typically mature a few years later than females), and (c) the resulting increased lateralization of brain functions in boys compared with girls (Levy, 1976). In addition, cognitive style, specifically predisposition toward field dependence or field independence (Wilkins, Oltman, Raskin, & Karp, 1959), was found to affect performance on spatial-perception tasks, such as horizontality (De Lisi, 1983). Field dependence is the extent to which individuals rely on bodily cues rather than visual referents. Individuals who rely on visual referents are field dependent and are expected to have more difficulty with horizontality tasks. More females are field dependent than field independent.

Psychosocial explanations emphasize early socializing influences, such as number of opportunities to explore the neighborhood, toys offered to children, and games and activities that put females at a disadvantage when performing spatial tasks, such as horizontality (Etaugh, 1983; Liben, 1991; Signorella, Jamison, & Krupa, 1989). Another psychosocial influence that may contribute to the poor performance of adult females is their sex role concept, which differs from males' sex role concept (Bem, 1974); boys and girls attribute different psychological traits to themselves. Researchers have found that a masculine sex role concept leads to increased confidence in performing horizontality tasks correctly (Kalichman, 1989). A third important psychosocial explanation for females' inferior performance on the horizontality tasks is that females lack adequate knowledge of principles that govern physical phenomena (Liben & Golbeck, 1980, 1984).

Several researchers have attempted to train adult women in the horizontality and verticality tasks (Kelly & Kelly, 1977; Liben, 1978; Liben & Golbeck, 1980, 1984; Roberts & Chaperon, 1989; Signorella & Jamison, 1978). The training method involved imparting the knowledge' of physical principles to the participants as well as demonstrating the correct answer with a real bottle, half filled with colored water, tilted to the appropriate angle. In a few studies females did improve substantially in their horizontality performance; however, none of these training studies was successful in eliminating gender differences in performance. These results add strength to the argument that there are biological underpinnings of the observed differences in the performance of males and females in the Piagetian Euclidean task.

Previous researchers have consistently found that gender is related to horizontality performance; however, there are other variables (i.e., field dependence) that may have confounded the observed relationships between gender and spatial performance. One question I attempted to address in this study was whether gender maintained its relationship with performance after I controlled for other significant variables. The second question was whether gender was an important predictor of posttest performance after training was introduced as a regressor. Other researchers have explained the poor performance of women as resulting from a lack of competence in dealing with space (Liben, 1991). In this study I attempted to assess the importance of several biological and psychosocial variables for performance on spatial tasks.

METHOD

Participants

The participants were 122 undergraduate students (35 men, 87 women) between 19 and 23 years old who were enrolled in introductory educational psychology courses at Rutgers University. They were awarded three class experimental participation credits for participating in this study.

Materials

The pretest contained seven paper-and-pencil, square-water-bottle items. In four of the items the outlines of the bottles tilted at 30° and 60° to the right and left: in two items the bottles were positioned horizontally; and in one item the bottle was upright. The figures of the bottles were displayed as resting on a horizontal surface so that the participants would have a remote reference frame for orienting their water lines (De Lisi, 1983).

Knowledge of physical principles was assessed by asking students to indicate how they knew where to place the waterline in the pretest and what principle they used.

A Portable Rod and Frame Test (PRFT; Witkins, Oltman, Raskin, & Karp, 1959) was used to measure the participants' field dependence. Four tilts of the frame and rod were used.

The square-bottle-training test consisted of the seven pretest items, but real square bottles were used.

The age at maturation measure (Sanders & Soares, 1986) was used to record the age of the participants at sexual maturation.

Bem's (1974) Sex Role Inventory was used to measure the participants' perceived masculinity, femininity, and androgyneity.

The Spatial Experience Inventory (Signorella, Krupa, Jamison, & Lyons, 1986) was used to measure the participants' previous spatial activities.

Design and Procedure

The initial sample consisted of 122 participants. Participants who failed two or more of the pretest items (22 men, 68 women) were randomly assigned to one of the three groups (the rule group, the graduated-instructions group, and the control group). Each group had 30 participants and a near equal proportion of men and women. Training for the rule group consisted of their being told the correct rule (for instance, the explication of the principle of gravity and how it affects water). The graduated-instruction group was offered the same information. However, the feedback was in steps of increasing specificity to the criterion response. There were seven levels of instruction (1 = "Your response was incorrect. Can you try again"; 7 = actual demonstration of the correct answer). The control group was not trained. All tests were individually administered.

The participants were then handed the sex-typing measure, the spatial experiential measure, the age at puberty scale, and the vocabulary test, one at a time. The instructions for each were read aloud, and the students had an opportunity to ask questions for clarification. Finally, the participants were tested on the PRFT. There was no immediate posttest administered.

After 1 month the participants were retested on the horizontality test. The horizontality test was scored in terms of the angle of deviation from the horizontal across all the items. The amount of training that the graduated-instructions group needed was also measured. A point was given each time a participant had to be given an additional instruction. The range for each item was 0 to 7 points. A score of 0 indicated that the participant did not need any instruction in performing the task to the criterion level, and a score of 7 indicated that the participant needed all seven instructions to perform the task to criterion level.

RESULTS

Pretest Analysis

Ninety participants failed the task (22 men, 68 women). Initially the patterns of correlation coefficients among all the variables included in the study were examined separately for men and women. There was no evidence for substantial group differences beyond those expected by chance, given the number of correlations compared.

A hierarchical multiple regression analysis was conducted in which significant variables from the group that had failed the pretest were entered. Order of entry (except for sex) was based on the consistency of the relationship in previous research findings. Field dependence was entered first; it explained 23% of the total variance in pretest performance. Knowledge contributed an increment of 10% in variance in pretest performance (that is, when field dependence was controlled for). Masculine sex role concepts accounted for an additional 6% in variance in pretest performance. The most important finding was that gender was significantly related to pretest score after controlling for all the other variables. It added 12% to the variance in pretest scores even with all the other significant variables partialed out.

Table 1. Factors Contributing to Variance in Posttest Scores

Factor	R^2	R^2 Change	F
FD	.17	.17	32.15(*)
Age	.18	.01	1.11
Knowledge	.22	.04	6.17(*)
Sex role	.25	.03	4.53
SA	.27	.02	2.14
Pretest	.30	.03	3.33
Sex	.30	.00	1.12
Group	.43	.13	27.63(*)
Instructions	.49	.06	15.16(*)

Note: FD = field dependence; age = age at sexual maturation; knowledge = knowledge of physical principles; sex role = masculine sex role concept; SA = spatial experience; pretest = pretest score. sex = sex of participant; group = experimental group; instructions = number needed to successfully complete an item.

(*) $p < .01$.

Posttest Analysis

Next, a hierarchical multiple regression analysis was conducted with the posttest horizontality performance as the dependent variable and the pretest scores as a covariate, and all the variables were entered in the same order as in the previous analysis. However, this time the scores for the experimental groups and the training scores were also included in the analysis.

Field dependence explained 17% of the variance. Knowledge and sex role concept were significantly related, but they contributed less to posttest variance in scores than to pretest variance in scores. Sex was an insignificant variable in posttest performance. Whether participants had received training seems to be one of the most important variables in determining horizontality scores. It added 12% of the variance in posttest scores (see Table 1). The effect of the number of instructions needed to successfully complete an item on the training task on posttest performance may actually be underestimated in this instance because several individuals in the training group had reached criterion performance in the posttest.

DISCUSSION

In the literature on horizontality tasks, one of the most consistently found group differences is in the performances of males and females. A sex difference favoring males in the horizontality task has been found across most cultures and disciplines of study (Barna & O'Connell, 1967; De Lisi, Parameswaran, & McGillicuddy-De Lisi, 1989; Kalichman, 1986, 1988; Kelly & Kelly, 1977; Myers & Hensley, 1984; Ohuche, 1984; Roberts, 1989). In this sample, the men were significantly more likely than the women to complete the pretest successfully.

Explanations as to why some individuals fail the horizontality test center on field dependence and lack of knowledge of the physical principles underlying horizontality. Previous investigators have found that performance on the horizontality task is highly correlated with performance on the rod and frame task and embedded figures task, which purport to measure the level of field dependence of the individual (De Lisi, 1983; Liben, 1978; Scholl, 1989). Both tasks require the participant to disregard the proximal frame of reference and concentrate on a distal one. However, these tasks do not measure the same construct. Some researchers have pointed out that with training, participants improve on the horizontality task, whereas performance on the field-dependence measures are more resistant to training. In this particular study, the initial horizontality scores were significantly correlated with field dependence, and this relationship was only slightly reduced when posttest horizontality scores were used as the dependent variable. The amount of gain that the participants manifested with training was limited by their cognitive style.

The knowledge that water maintains its own level because of gravity has been associated with better performance on water–level tasks (Golbeck, 1986; Liben, 1978; Liben & Golbeck, 1980; Linn & Pulos, 1983). The participants who knew the principle performed better on the pretest than the participants who did not know the principle. This confirmed the results of earlier studies. Thus, both field dependence and the knowledge of the physical principle underlying the waterlevel task affected pretest performance.

Previous researchers found that field dependence and knowledge correlated significantly, so that participants who were field dependent were often not able to vocalize the principle behind the action of water in containers (Mowrer-Popiel, 1991). In this study, lack of knowledge about physical phenomena was altered with training, but the success of the training depended on field dependence.

One of the most controversial issues in the field of spatial-ability testing is the contribution of biological and psychosocial variables to performance. This issue is also reflected in the literature on horizontality tasks (Jamison & Signorella, 1980; Kalichman, 1986, 1988, 1989; Meehan & Overton, 1986; Signorella & Jamison, 1978). The participant's age at sexual maturation has been proposed to affect performance on tests of spatial ability (Harris, Hanley, & Best, 1977; Roberts, 1989). When field dependence was entered first, the age at maturation was not related to pretest performance.

Sherman (1967) and Signorella et al. (1986) claimed that the sex difference in performance on horizontality tasks was the result of different spatial activities engaged in by boys and girls. In this study, the activity that the participant habitually reported to be engaged in did not seem to affect performance on the horizontality test. None of the activity ratings (masculine, feminine, and neutral) were related significantly to the pretest. The kind of activity the participant reported to be involved in did depend on his or her sex; that is, the men indulged in more masculine activities, and the women indulged in more feminine activities.

The only stable psychosocial factor that seemed to have some influence on performance on horizontality tasks was the rating of the participants on masculine adjectives. A masculine self-concept was associated with better performance on the horizontality test in the pretest, but not in the posttest.

The participants in the training groups improved their scores between the pretest and the posttest on the water-bottle task. This improvement was reflected by the tact that, when pretest and sex were controlled for, training explained 12% of the posttest variance.

Previous studies have demonstrated the value of a structure within which participants learn a new skill (Cole, 1975; Rogoff, Markin, & Gilbride, 1984). Vygotsky (1978) argued that, with a friendly expert, novices can perform tasks that they cannot do by themselves. Vygotsky also claimed that the amount of training needed to perform a task was a better measure of a skill than independent problem solving. The number of instructions participants needed to perform to criterion level contributed to explaining posttest performance even after controlling for all the other significant variables. The effects of the number of instructions on posttest performance may have actually been lowered because several participants performed to criterion level on the posttest.

One major drawback of this study is that many variables were incorporated. There is, currently, no existing model that integrates these variables into a comprehensive framework toward understanding performance on horizontality tasks. This study, however, could be a starting point for new explorations in the area.

There were too few men in each of the experimental groups; therefore, the gender differences on some tasks could have been masked. This possibility holds not only for this report but also for other reports on spatial ability. However, Liben (1990) emphasized that it is better to incorporate men who are available into studies on horizontality than to ignore them. Both males and females fail the horizontality task.

Future researchers must attempt to unravel the components of cognitive style that make such style an important factor in performances on horizontality tasks. In future training studies, researchers can explore the specific ways field dependence affects performance (e.g., perhaps field independence makes it easier for individuals to acquire knowledge of the principle of gravity spontaneously), and they can aim training to remedy those facets of performance that need improvement.

In addition, researchers should study the question of how these various antecedent biological and psychosocial factors interact to determine horizontality performance. A detailed investigation could be undertaken of how sex roles and age at sexual maturity interact with the social and emotional process of understanding space.

In this study I chose to ignore all of those interactions because they would pose too broad a field to study in one research project. The results of this study may add to the existing efforts to understand children's and adults' performance on spatial tasks.

Address correspondence to Gowri Parameswaran, Department of Psychology, Southwest Missouri State University, 901 South National Ave, Springfield, MO 65804-0095.

CRITICAL THINKING QUESTIONS

1. Field dependence involves the ability to separate an object from its surroundings. The horizontality task involves predicting where the water line would fall on a tilted glass. Why would field dependence influence the ability to perform on the horizontality task?

2. Parameswaran states that previous research on gender differences in the horizontal water level task has shown that "masculine sex role concept leads to increased confidence in performing horizontality tasks correctly." This statement is based upon a correlation. Are there any problems with inferring causality on the basis of such data? What are the possible alternatives to the causal model implied by this statement?

3. In the Parameswaran experiment, success on the horizontality task was assessed via a 7-point scale. Therefore, participants could receive a range of scores rather than a correct/incorrect score. What is the advantage of structuring the scoring in this fashion?

REFERENCES

Barna. J. D., & O'Connell, D. C. (1967). Perception of horizontality as a function of age and stimulus settings. *Perception and Motor Skills, 25,* 70–72.

Bem, S. (1974). *Bem Sex Role Inventory professional manual.* Palo Alto, CA: Consulting Psychologists Press.

Cole, J. D. (1975). An ethnographic psychology of cognition. In R. W. Brislin (Ed.), *Cross-cultural perspectives on learning* (pp. 51–68). New York: Wiley.

De Lisi, R. (1983). Developmental and individual differences in children's representation of the horizontal coordinate. *Merrill-Palmer Quarterly 29*(2), 179–196.

De Lisi, R., Parameswaran, G., & McGillicuddy-De Lisi, A. V. (1989). Age and sex differences in representation of horizontality among school children in India. *Perceptual and Motor Skills, 68,* 739–746.

Etaugh, C. (1983). The influences of environmental factors on sex differences in children's play. In M. B. Liss (Ed.), *Social and cognitive skills* (pp. 52–83). San Diego: Academic Press.

Golbeck, S. L. (1986). The role of physical content in Piagetian spatial tasks: Sex differences in spatial knowledge? *Journal of Research in Science Teaching, 23*(4), 365-376.

Harris, L., Hanley, M., & Best, N. (1977). Conservation of horizontality: Sex differences in 6th grade and college students. In R. H. Smart (Ed.), *Readings in child development and relationships* (pp. 375-387). New York: Macmillan.

Jamison, W., & Signorella, M. L. (1980). Sex typing and spatial ability: The association between masculinity and success on Piaget's water level task. *Sex Roles, 6,* 345–353.

Kalichman, S. C. (1986). Horizontality as a function of sex and academic major. *Perceptual and Motor Skills, 63,* 903–906.

Kalichman, S. C. (1988). Individual differences in water level task performance: A component-skill analysis. *Developmental Review, 8,* 273–295.

Kalichman, S. C. (1989). Sex roles and sex differences in adult spatial performance. *The Journal of Genetic Psychology, 150*(1), 93–100.

Kelly, J. T., & Kelly, G. N. (1977). Perception of horizontality by male and female college students. *Perceptual and Motor Skills, 44,* 724–726.

Levy, J. (1976). Cerebral lateralization and spatial ability. *Behavior Genetics, 6,* 171–188.

Liben, L. S. (1978). Performance on Piagetian spatial tasks as a function of sex, field dependence and training. *Merrill-Palmer Quarterly, 24,* 97–110.

Liben, L. S. (1990). Piagetian water level task: Looking beneath the surface. In L. S. Liben (Ed.), *Annals of child development* (pp. 552–573). London: Jessica Kingsley Publishers.

Liben, L. S. (1991). Adults' performance on horizontality tasks: Conflicting frames of reference. *Developmental Psychology, 27*(2), 285–294.

Liben, L. S., & Golbeck, S. L. (1980). Sex difference in performance on Piagetian tasks: Differences in competence or performance? *Child Development, 51,* 594–597.

Liben, L. S., & Golbeck, S. L. (1984). Sex differences in performance on Piagetian spatial tasks: Sex related differences and knowledge of physical phenomena. *Developmental Psychology, 20,* 595–606.

Linn, M. G., & Peterson, A. C. (1985). Emergence and characterization of spatial ability: A meta-analysis. *Child Development, 56,* 1479–1498.

Linn, M. G., & Pulos, R. (1983). Sex differences in knowledge of physical principles. *Journal of Research in Science Teaching, 20*(2), 169–176.

Meehan, A. M., & Overton, W. F. (1986). Gender differences in expectancies for success and performance on Piagetian spatial tasks. *Merrill-Palmer Quarterly, 32*(4), 427–441.

Mowrer-Popiel, E. (1991). Adolescent and adult comprehension of horizontality as a function of cognitive style, training and task difficulty. *Dissertation Abstracts International, 51*(7–A), 2322.

Myers, R. L., & Hensley, M. N. (1984). Cognitive gender, style, and self-report as predictors of Piaget's water-level task. *The Journal of Genetic Psychology, 144,* 179–183.

Ohuche, L. N. (1984). Performance on the coordinate reference system: Are gender differences universal? *Journal of Cross-Cultural Psychology, 15*(3), 285–296.

Piaget, J., & Inhelder, B. (1956). *The child's conception of space.* London: Routledge and Kegan Paul.

Roberts, M. (1989). Robustness of sex differences in horizontality. Unpublished manuscript.

Roberts, M., & Chaperon, P. (1989). Cognitive and exemplary modeling on the Piagetian water-level task. *International Journal of Behavior Development, 12,* 453–473.

Rogoff, B., Markin, C., & Gilbride, K. (1984). Interaction with babies as guidance in development. In B. Rogoff & J. V. Wertsch (Eds.), *New directions in child development* (pp. 21–68). New York: Jossey-Bass.

Sanders, B., & Soares, M. P. (1986). Sexual maturation and spatial ability in college students. *Developmental Psychology, 22*(2), 199–203.

Scholl, M. J. (1989). The relation between horizontality and rod and frame and vestibular navigational performance. *Journal of Experimental Psychology: Learning, Memory and Cognition, 15*(1), 110–125.

Sherman, J. A. (1967). Problems of sex differences in space perception and aspects of intellectual functioning. *Psychological Review, 74,* 290–299.

Signorella, K., & Jamison, T. (1978). Sex differences in the correlation among the FD, spatial ability, sex-role orientation and performance on Piaget's water level task. *Developmental Psychology, 14,* 689–690.

Signorella, M., Jamison, W., & Krupa, M. H. (1989). Predicting spatial performance from gender stereotyping in activity and self-concept. *Developmental Psychology, 25*(1), 89–95.

Signorella, M. L., Krupa, M. H., Jamison, W., & Lyons, N. (1986). A short version of the spatial activities questionnaire. *Sex Roles, 14,* 475–479.

Thomas, H., & Jamison, W. (1981 a). A test of the x-linked genetic hypothesis for sex differences on Piaget's water level task. *Developmental Review, 1,* 274–283.

Thomas, H., & Jamison, W. (1981b). Genetic mediation of the sex difference in horizontality—A rejoinder. *Developmental Review, 1,* 296–299.

Vygotsky, L. S. (1978). *Mind in society.* Cambridge, MA: Harvard University Press.

Witkins, H. A., Oltman, P. K., Raskin, E., & Karp, S. A. (1959). *Manual for Embedded Figures Test.* Palo Alto, CA: Consulting Psychologists Press.

8

Memory and Information Processing

Memory and Aging

John C. Cavanaugh

The common perception of memory loss during aging is simplistic since there are certain aspects such as recognition ability and long-term memory that only change minimally. It is only in such areas as attention and sensory perception that aging takes its toll. Working memory, on the other hand, may generally decline with age but not as much in the case of experts in their field. People's beliefs and feelings about aging also affect their capacity to age successfully. In such case, their beliefs become self-fulfilling prophecies as they become what they feel would happen.

G rowing older is difficult on a personal level for many people. In part, the concern and anxiety people feel result from societal attitudes that favor youth, especially for women. However, such feelings also result from misconceptions about what aging entails on a personal level, which in turn result from a lack of accurate information about the psychological aspects of aging.

One area in which personal concerns are especially prominent is memory. Perhaps no other psychological criterion is used more to check how well we are functioning. Likewise, no other cognitive skill is as pervasive in everything we do, from remembering how to brush our teeth in the morning to remembering to set the alarm when we go to bed at night.

Reprinted from National Forum, Volume 78, Number 2 (Spring 1998). Copyright by John C. Cavanaugh. By permission of the publishers.

In this article, I will summarize briefly the research literature on memory and aging. In particular, I will focus on the complex processes we use to acquire, store, and remember information, the role of personal beliefs about memory and memory change, and the place of memory in clinical testing. Readers interested in learning more about cognitive processes and aging should consult the book *Perspectives on Cognitive Changes in Adulthood and Late Life* edited by Blanchard-Fields and Hess (McGraw-Hill [1996]). Of course, memory is but one aspect of the broader arena of psychological changes with age; readers wishing to learn more may wish to consult my book *Adult Development and Aging* (3rd ed., Brooks/Cole [1997]).

PROCESSING AND REMEMBERING INFORMATION

One of the most commonly held beliefs about aging is that memory inevitably declines. Unfortunately, this view, though somewhat correct, is much too simplistic. The reason is that getting information into our heads in such a way that we can remember it on demand later is the result of a series of complex processes: sensory memory, attention, working memory, short-term memos, and long-term memory. Psychologists who study these processes in the context of aging have discovered that some of them change dramatically with age, whereas others seem to change very little.

Sensory memory is the earliest step in information processing, the step in which incoming information is first registered. Although very large amounts of information can be taken in at this step, it is lost quickly unless we pay attention to it. For instance, try drawing both sides of a U.S. quarter; even though we see these coins every day, and the information is registered, because most of us do not pay enough attention, we are not very good at this task. Researchers have shown that the amount of visual information we can handle at one time declines with age, as does the speed with which people can identify target information within this information.

Attention is an extremely important aspect of information processing; indeed, without it, the odds of remembering a specific piece of information drop dramatically. Psychologists study attention by focusing on three major types: selective attention, divided attention, and sustained attention. Selective attention entails being able to pick out a particular target or piece of information from a larger display (for example, finding all the e's on this page or the cars that may be likely to pull out in front of you in a busy intersection). As people grow older, the speed with which they can accomplish such tasks slows down a great deal—their reaction times slow considerably, sometimes by a factor of 100 percent, depending on the task. Reaction-time slowing is especially dramatic when the information presented and the necessary response are complex, which is typically the case when driving a car. Only when people know exactly where to look ahead of time (such as expert birdwatchers knowing where in a tree a tufted titmouse is most likely to be) are these reaction time differences not as great. Older adults are also much less able than younger ones to do two effortful things at the same time (such as listen to a physician's report and write down notes simultaneously) unless they have had substantial amounts of practice in the exact tasks they have to perform together. Older adults also are not as good at identifying target information in tasks requiring sustained attention (such as looking at gauges and waiting for malfunction warnings).

These age-related changes in attention, especially those relating to reaction time, have important practical implications. Most important, they indicate that many of the basic cognitive processes essential for driving a car decline as people age. Slower reaction times mean that older drivers are slower in responding to emergency situations. Problems with selective attention—failures to detect important information—are reflected in accident victims' reports that "I never saw the other car." Combined with declines in vision, especially concerning the drop in people's ability to see in low-light conditions, such changes underlie the well-known reluctance of older people about driving at night. Additionally, attentional problems also result in accidents around the home, such as tripping and falling over area rugs or other objects. One should keep these issues in mind when helping older adults arrange items in their homes.

Working memory is another key aspect of information processing. Working memory refers to the processes and structures involved in holding information in mind and simultaneously using that information (sometimes with incoming information) to solve a problem, make a decision, or learn new information. Cooking is a good example of working memory—you need to monitor all the cooking rates of the various aspects of the meal, check for doneness, and get the timing right so that everything is ready at the same time. Unlike sensory memory, which has a very large capacity, working memory has a very limited capacity. Working memory operates much like a juggler who can keep only a relatively few things in the air simultaneously. It works as our mental scratchpad: As long as we are using the information, it is active; when we stop using it, it is gone. This is why we learn at an early age to rehearse information such as phone numbers that we need to use right after we look them up in the phonebook—if we didn't, we would forget the number.

Although we do not yet know the extent of the change, there is substantial evidence that in general the capacity of working memory declines with age, as does the efficacy and efficiency of rehearsal. However, the picture is more complicated in areas in which people are experts. On the one hand, expertise greatly reduces age differences in the speed with which information can be retrieved into working memory, but the efficiency of its subsequent use is unchanged. Thus, although practice may help people retrieve information faster, it may not help them use it more effectively.

Short-term memory is what first comes to many people's minds when they think about memory—the ability to remember information from a few minutes to a few hours. Questions such as, "What did you have for breakfast this morning?" require short-term memory when asked of someone in the middle of the afternoon. Short-term memory is generally tested in two ways: through recall tests, in which people are asked to remember something with no hints (such as the breakfast question above), and through recognition tests, in which people are presented various options and asked to select the correct one. In general, people's ability to remember information in situations requiring recall declines with age, whereas people's recognition ability tends to remain fairly stable. However, older adults can learn to use compensatory strategies, such as lists and calendars, to improve their performance in recall situations.

Long-term memory refers to remembering information learned and stored years earlier, such as autobiographical events and general knowledge (for example, facts about George Washington learned in school). A commonly-held stereotype of aging is that older adults remain good at remembering information from the past. In this case, the stereotype is largely accurate: Older adults' ability to remember such information does not normally decline.

SELF-EVALUATIONS OF MEMORY ABILITY

Despite data in key aspects of information processing to the contrary, most people believe that memory declines with age and that there is nothing which can be done about it. This lack of complete correspondence with research data is important. If people believe that memory declines inevitably, they may not engage in practices that could help them remember; in short, they may subject themselves to a self-fulfilling prophecy. Belief in inevitable decline leads to a failure to compensate, which leads to poorer performance, which leads to confirmation of the original belief. (Of course, the converse is true as well: people who think they have good memories may engage in appropriate compensatory behaviors to ensure good performance.)

Since the mid-1970s, my own research has focused on these belief-performance relations. In a paper with Jack Feldman and Christopher Hertzog, I discuss how self-evaluations of memory are quite complex, and are based not only on what we know about our own memory and performance, but also on how we view ourselves in general, our personal theories about how memory works, what we remember from past evaluations, and our attributions and judgments of our effectiveness as rememberers, ("Metamemory as Social Cognition: Reconceptualizing What Memory Questionnaires Assess," *Review of General Psychology,* 2:48–65 [1998]).

Older adults seem to know less than younger adults about the internal workings of memory and its capacity, view memory as less stable, expect that memory will deteriorate with age, perceive that they have less control over memory, and believe that trying to do something to help is useless. People's beliefs about how well they will perform a specific memory task (termed memory self-efficacy) is especially key. Memory self-efficacy is important in understanding how people behave when confronted with a novel memory situation. Individuals with high memory self-efficacy are likely to attempt the task and exert more effort at it than people with low memory self-efficacy. Such differences in efficacy may underlie some of the age-related performance differences uncovered in memory research. Although there is not much data as of yet, it is also possible that one effective approach to memory intervention may be focusing on people's belief systems; indeed, this very approach underlies cognitive behavior therapy, one of the most successful psychological interventions for depression.

CLINICAL ISSUES AND MEMORY

Because memory is such a ubiquitious part of our daily lives, people tend to use it as their yardstick for determining how well they are aging (that is, if their "mind" is still okay). Reliance on memory as the key indicator probably reflects a fear of dementia, especially Alzheimer's disease, which involves the progressive destruction of cognitive abilities.

It turns out that in general people are on the right track; clinicians use a variety of memory tests to differentiate normal from abnormal memory aging. As we have seen, many normative changes take place in memory as people grow old, such as in attention, working memory, and recall performance. Still, some aspects of memory processing show little normative change, such as recognition performance and long-term memory. By focusing on these latter aspects, and testing for changes in them, clinicians are able to identify performance patterns that deviate from the norm. This is the basic strategy used in clinical memory testing.

A thorough clinical work-up includes standardized neuropsychological batteries (which test a wide variety of cognitive functions), neuropsychological tests (such as computed tomography [CT] and magnetic resonance imaging [MRI]), and blood tests. Only by combining the results of all of these tests are clinicians able to diagnose various types of cognitive problems. Still, it is often difficult to tell the difference between normal and abnormal aging; there is no magic number of times a person has to forget something in order for the performance to be classified as abnormal.

SUMMARY AND CONCLUSIONS

Despite stereotypes of global, inevitable deterioration of memory with age, psychological research indicates that the actual pattern is far more complex. Additionally, people's beliefs about their own memory and how it changes over time further complicate the picture. Telling the difference between normal and abnormal memory aging is grounded in the normative patterns of change, but must be done in a thorough and systematic manner. Compensations for some types of declines are possible, but they do not eliminate the entire difference.

The aging of the baby-boom generation will present important challenges for psychologists. Making sure that people have accurate information about memory aging will be an important goal in setting the record straight and in combating inaccurate stereotypes.

John C. Cavanaugh, Ph.D., is Vice Provost for Academic Programs and Planning at the University of Delaware. He is the author of numerous articles and books on aging. His forthcoming book, edited with Susan Krauss Whilbourne, is Gerontology: An Interdisciplinary Perspective, *published by Oxford University Press. He is a former president of the Adult Development and Aging Division (20) of the American Psychological Association.*

CRITICAL THINKING QUESTIONS

1. Cavanaugh states that people's beliefs about the age-related changes associated with memory influence their ability to deal with these changes. Discuss how this link between beliefs and memory performance operates.

2. People who are experts in a particular area (e.g., bird watching) show lesser degrees of age-related impairment on related tasks. In this case, experience (nurture) and biological changes in the brain (nature) are interacting to influence performance. Discuss how being an expert might be useful in a memory task.

9

Intelligence and Creativity

Genetics and Intelligence

Robert Plomin

Genetics of Childhood Disorders, part 3

Intelligence or general cognitive ability clearly is a family characteristic. Studies show that heritability accounts for a considerable amount of the total variance in general cognitive ability scores. Research also indicates that different cognitive abilities are significantly influenced by the same genetic factors. Heritability of intelligence and other complex dimensions may be attributed to multiple genes with different but minor effect instead of just one gene with a major impact.

Genetic research has made important discoveries about intelligence during the past few decades. To outline some of these findings, I won't spend space on the measurement of intelligence except to say that what I mean by intelligence is general cognitive ability defined as *g*. All reliable and valid tests of cognitive ability intercorrelate at a modest level—*g* is what they have in common, *g* is often assessed as a total score across diverse cognitive tests as in intelligence (IQ) tests, although it is more accurately indexed by an unrotated **principal** component that best reflects what is in common among the tests. Nearly all genetic data have been obtained using measures developed

Journal of the American Academy of Child and Adolescent Psychiatry, June 1999 v38 i6 p786(3).

from this psychometric perspective, primarily IQ tests. One new direction for genetic research on intelligence is to investigate other measures such as information-processing and more direct measures of brain function such as evoked potentials, positron emission tomographic scans, and functional magnetic resonance imaging and to explain how these measures relate to g.

g clearly runs in families. The correlations for first-degree relatives living together average 0.43 for more than 8,000 parent-offspring pairs and 0.47 for more than 25,000 pairs of siblings. However, g might run in families for reasons of nurture or of nature. In studies involving more than 10,000 pairs of twins, the average g correlations are 0.85 for identical twins and 0.60 for same-sex fraternal twins. These twin data suggest a genetic effect size (heritability) that explains about half of the total variance in g scores.

Adoption studies also yield estimates of substantial heritability. For example, identical twins reared apart are almost as similar for g as identical twins reared together. Adoption studies of other first-degree relatives also indicate substantial heritability, as illustrated below by recent results from the Colorado Adoption Project (CAP). Model-fitting analyses based on dozens of adoption and twin studies estimate that about half of the total variance can be attributed to genetic factors. Genetic influence on g is not only statistically significant, it is also substantial, especially when compared to other research in the behavioral sciences that rarely explains 5% of the variance. Genetic research has moved beyond the question of heritability of intelligence to investigate developmental changes, multivariate relations among cognitive abilities, and specific genes responsible for the heritability of g. These 3 issues will now be addressed.

When Francis Galton first studied twins in 1876, he investigated the extent to which the similarity of twins changes over the course of development. Other early twin studies of g were also developmental, but this developmental perspective faded from genetic research until recent years. One of the most interesting findings about g is that heritability increases steadily from infancy (20%) to childhood (40%) to adulthood (60%). For example, a recent study of twins aged 80 years and older reported a heritability of about 60.

The 20-year longitudinal CAP confirms this finding using the adoption design. CAP is a 25-year study of 245 children separated from their biological parents at birth and adopted in the first month of life. Correlations are shown between g scores of the biological parents and their adopted-away children, the adoptive parents and their adopted children, and nonadoptive or control parents and their children matched to the adoptive families. Correlations between nonadoptive parents and children increase from less than 0.20 in infancy to about 0.20 in middle childhood and to about 0.30 in adolescence. The correlations between biological mothers and their adopted-away children follow a similar pattern, indicating that parent-offspring resemblance for g is due to genetic factors. In contrast, parent-offspring correlations for adoptive parents and their adopted children hover around zero, which suggests that family environment shared by parents and offspring does not contribute importantly to parent-offspring resemblance for g.

Why does heritability of *g* increase during the life span? Perhaps completely new genes come to affect *g* as more sophisticated cognitive processes develop. A more likely possibility is that relatively small genetic effects early in life snowball during development, creating larger and larger phenotypic effects, perhaps as individuals select or create environments that foster their genetic propensities.

There is more, however, to cognitive abilities than *g*. In the widely accepted hierarchical model of cognitive abilities, specific cognitive abilities include components such as spatial, verbal, speed-of-processing, and memory abilities, each indexed by what is in common among several tests of each ability. Less is known about the genetic and environmental origins of individual differences in specific cognitive abilities, but they also appear to show substantial genetic influence, although less than *g*.

A surprising finding concerning specific cognitive abilities is that multivariate genetic analyses indicate that the same genetic factors largely influence different abilities. What this finding means concretely is that if a specific gene were found that is associated with verbal ability, the gene would also be expected to be associated with spatial ability and other specific cognitive abilities. This finding is surprising because it goes against the tide of the popular modular theory of cognitive neuroscience that assumes that cognitive processes are specific and relatively independent of one another. The multivariate genetic results are consistent with a top-down model in which genetic effects of *g* pervade a broad range of cognitive processes. An even more surprising finding in 4 out of 4 studies is that genetic effects on measures of school achievement overlap almost completely with genetic effects on *g*. The converse of this finding of genetic overlap is equally interesting. Although genetics accounts for the overlap between school achievement and *g*, discrepancies between school achievement and *g*, often used to describe underachievers, are largely environmental in origin.

Heritability of complex dimensions such as *g* seems likely to be due to multiple genes of varying but small effect size rather than a single gene that has a major effect. Genes in such multiple-gene systems are called quantitative trait loci (QTLs). Unlike single-gene effects like PKU that are necessary and sufficient for the development of a disorder, QTLs contribute interchangeably and additively like probabilistic risk factors. Traditional methods for identifying single-gene effects are unlikely to succeed in identifying QTLs.

A QTL study applying new genetic approaches to *g* yielded a replicated association in a study comparing groups of children of high *g* and children of average *g*. The gene is insulin-like growth factor-2 receptor (IGF2R) on chromosome 6, which has recently been shown to be especially active in brain regions most involved in learning and memory. The frequency of one of the alleles was twice as high in 2 groups of children with high *g* compared with 2 groups of children with average g (about 30% versus 15%).

Identifying replicable QTLs associated with *g* will make it possible to address questions about development, differential diagnosis, and gene-environment interplay through the use of measured genotypes rather than indirect inferences about heritable influence based on familial resemblance. Such QTLs will also provide discrete windows through which to view neurophysiological pathways between genes and cognitive development. As is the case with most important advances, identifying genes for cognitive abilities and disabilities will also raise new ethical issues. These concerns must be taken seriously, but they are based largely on misconceptions about genetic research on complex traits that are influenced by multiple genes as well as multiple environmental factors.

Dr. Plomin is Professor, Social, Genetic and Developmental Psychiatry Research Centre, Institute of Psychiatry, London.

WEB SITES OF INTEREST

http://205.153.39.175/programs/sfkids/showarchive/sfkc.98.01.02.html
http://www.nhgri.nih.gov/HGP/HGP_goals/5yrplan.html

CRITICAL THINKING QUESTIONS

1. Heritability studies such as those cited by Plomin often involve comparing concordance on a particular trait for fraternal and identical twins raised together or raised apart, with the assumption that higher concordance rates for identical twins implies a stronger genetic influence. Implicit in this type of study is the assumption that being raised in different families results in a different environment. Discuss how active and evocative genotype environment correlations might influence the environments twins are raised in, and how this might impact the heritability estimate.

2. The research Plomin cites in his paper indicates that genetic influences on intelligence are relatively strong and increase with age, while the correlations between adoptive parents' and their children's intelligence is close to zero. Does this mean that the environment has little influence on intelligence? Why or why not?

ADDITIONAL READINGS

Chorney MJ, Chorney K, Seese Net al. (1998). A quantitative trait locus (QTL) associated with cognitive ability in children. *Psychol Sci* 9:159–166.

Plomin R, DeFries JC (1998), The genetics of cognitive abilities and disabilities. *Sci Am* 278(5):62–69.

Plomin R, DeFries JC, McClearn GE, Rutter M (1997), *Behavioral Genetics,* 3rd ed. New York: Freeman.

Plomin R, Fulker DW, Corley R, DeFries JC (1997), Nature, nurture and cognitive development from 1 to 16 years: a parent-offspring adoption study. *Psychol Sci* 8:442–447.

Plomin R, Owen MJ, McGuffin P (1994), The genetic basis of complex human behaviors. *Science* 264:1733–1739.

Plomin R, Rutter M (1998), Child development, molecular genetics, and what to do with genes once they are found. *Child Dev* 69:1221–1240.

10

Language and Education

Effects of Neighborhood Socioeconomic Characteristics and Class Composition on Highly Competent Children

Stefania Maggi, Clyde Hertzman, Dafina Kohen, and Amedio D'Angiulli

The association has been widely established between early development, poor school performance, and increased risk for a variety of disadvantages later in life such as poor literacy abilities, low school achievement, grade failure, and poor employment opportunities (see Baydar, Brooks-Gunn, & Furstenberg, 1993; Darlington, Royce, Snipper, Murray, & Lazar, 1980; Hertzman, 1992; Power & Hertzman, 1997). Because of that association, researchers who want to understand the origins of poor school performance have been investigating the effects of family and neighborhood socioeconomic characteristics on the development of skills such as reading and mathematics. Several researchers have emphasized the fact that children from lower socioeconomic families who attend schools in less affluent neighborhoods tend to perform worse than do children from more affluent families, neighborhoods,

The Journal of Educational Research, Nov–Dec 2004, v98 i2 p109(6).

and schools (Brooks-Gunn, Klebanov, Liaw, & Spiker, 1993; Chase-Lansdale, Gordon, BrooksGunn, & Klebanov, 1997; Duncan & Brooks-Gunn, 1997; Haveman & Wolfe, 1995).

In Canada, gradients in the development of basic school-related competencies (e.g., reading and numeracy) that are based on family income and maternal education levels are evident in children as early as their first 5 years of life. Data from the National Longitudinal Survey of Children and Youth in Canada have shown that the proportion of children with low receptive verbal-ability scores rose front approximately 8% among the children of families with incomes in excess of $80,000 yearly to more than 35%, a five-fold difference, among those with incomes of less than $20,000 per year (Ross & Roberts, 1999). Our recent work conducted in Vancouver has shown that the development of early childhood preschool competencies varies enormously by the sociodemographic character of urban neighborhoods, such that the proportion of children of kindergarten age at risk for later difficulties in reading and numeracy ranges from 0% to 21% across the city's 23 planning neighborhoods (Hertztman, McLean, Kohen, Dunn, & Evans, 2002). When other dimensions of development (cognitive, physical, social, and emotional) are considered, the proportion of children with one or more developmental vulnerabilities varies from 6% to 38% across neighborhoods. Those data raise the concern that by the time children begin formal education in Grade 1, the proportion of children who are at risk for developing problems in reading and numeracy varies enormously according to the school neighborhood.

In affluent neighborhoods, a Grade 1 teacher with 30 children in the classroom can expect that few of the children have a cognitive delay and that no more than 3 or 4 children have any form of developmental vulnerability. In less affluent neighborhoods, a teacher who also has 30 children in a classroom may face more children who experience learning difficulties and more than 10 children who have some form of developmental delay (Hertzman et al., 2002).

Research has shown that neighborhood socioeconomic characteristics are associated with classroom composition (higher proportions of children at risk, larger class size, fewer available resources) that, in turn, may be related to the learning experiences of children at risk for academic difficulties (D'Agostino, 2000; Nye, Hedges, & Kostantopoulos, 2001). However, the learning difficulties of a few children may be associated not only with the academic trajectories of such children but also with those of children who, despite living in less affluent neighborhoods and attending schools with limited resources, have above-average academic performance. The learning experiences of the highly competent children may be compromised by the less stimulating academic climate created by a high proportion of children who face learning difficulties and by the lack of attention from a teacher who is focused on children who require additional support. Unfortunately, a limited number of researchers have explored that hypothesis.

Although some researchers did address the conditions that enable students who are on a path toward failure to significantly improve academic achievement (e.g., Cappella & Weinstein, 2000; Padron, Waxman, & Huang, 1999), to our knowledge, no one has explored how neighborhood socioeconomic characteristics and class composition are associated with the performance of highly competent children. In other words, educational literature is rich with studies on the conditions that hinder children's expected development and academic achievement; diminished performance of highly competent children, on the other hand, has never been studied. That omission is unfortunate because a highly competent child who later in her academic career becomes an average performer is clearly not achieving at her best potential, which, in turn, may indicate that her development has, to some extent, been hindered. Obviously, that outcome contradicts the principle of equal opportunity that informs educational practices in our schools.

Thus, we argued that the conditions that are involved in the failure of one to fully develop her or his potential are worthy of attention also for those children who, as early as kindergarten, show potential for becoming highly competent but are held back by the combination of factors at the school and neighborhood levels.

The novel contribution of this study is that we made a first attempt to direct attention to the following unexplored issue: a cross-sectional analysis of the differences between highly competent kindergarten (K), Grade 4 (G4), and Grade 7 (G7) students. We explored the extent to which those differences are associated with neighborhood socioeconomic characteristics and class composition.

METHOD

Sample and Procedure

Using cross-sectional data collected from schools in the Vancouver School District, we investigated the associations of neighborhood socioeconomic characteristics, classroom composition, and early cognitive and language development with school performance in reading and numeracy among K, G4, and G7 children. In February 2000, kindergarten teachers in 88 schools in the Vancouver School District completed the Early Development Instrument (EDI) questionnaire on all their pupils. The data, which included all public kindergarten classes in Vancouver, served as our measure of early development. It included approximately 97% of all Vancouver children of kindergarten age. For 78 of the schools (the remaining 10 schools did not have G4 and G7 classes), we obtained the G4 and G7 scores from the 1999/2000 Foundation Skills Assessments of Reading and Mathematics. We then used the neighborhood socioeconomic indicators to predict the proportion of highly competent children with above-average competencies and school performance, in K (with the EDI language and cognitive scores), G4, and G7 (with the FSA reading and numeracy scores).

Measures

The EDI (Janus & Offord, 2000) is an age-appropriate, teacher-completed checklist that examines how ready kindergarten children are for the elementary grades. The EDI is used to study populations of children in different communities to help communities assess how well they are supporting young children and their families. The EDI consists of five areas of competence based on indicators of children's school readiness: (a) physical health and well being, (b) social competence, (c) emotional maturity, (d) language and cognitive development, and (e) communication skills and general knowledge (Doherty, 1997; U.S. National Education Goals Panel, 1993). In the present study, we focus on the Language and Cognitive Development subscale because we expect that it is the subscale most closely associated with the FSA tests of reading and numeracy administered in G4 and G7 classrooms.

In 1998 and 1999, the EDI was normed on over 16,000 children nationwide. The instrument is a group-level measure: even though it was completed for each child, it was not designed as a diagnostic tool, and data are meant to be interpreted at a group level (i.e., for a whole class, a whole school, or a whole neighborhood). For the purposes of this study, children whose performance fell below the 10th percentile were considered at risk for learning difficulties in reading and numeracy, whereas children who performed above the 90th percentile were considered highly competent.

The FSA is a provincial test administered in British Columbia for the evaluation of reading and numeracy skills of school-aged children. The test is administered individually to all students, and scores are aggregated at the school level and publicly released in three categories: (a) proportion of schoolchildren who perform below expectations, (b) proportion of schoolchildren who meet expectations, and (c) proportion of schoolchildren who exceed expectations relative to other same-grade peers in the province. Scores are assigned by a representative sample of British Columbia teachers (approximately 550) who work in teams. Each team identifies an exemplary test that will be used as a reference when marking the remaining tests. Each test is then assigned to one of the following categories:

1. Meets expectations—level of performance at which a student meets or exceeds the widely held expectations for the test grade;

2. Exceeds expectations—level of a student's performance that is beyond that at which a teacher would state that the student has fully met the expectations of the test grade;

3. Not yet within expectations—level of a student's performance that has not attained the "meets expectations" standard.

The socioeconomic characteristics of the neighborhood catchment areas of the schools were obtained from the Vancouver School Disrict and are shown in Table 1 (see also for mean school percentage). We used class size, proportion of children in special education, and proportion of children at risk with respect to mathematics and reading to determine class composition. For K,

Table 1. School Socioeconomic Indicators for School Catchment Areas (N = 78)

Socioeconomic Indicator	M (%)	SD
Single-parent families	.17	.05
Home owners	.56	.14
Immigrants	.47	.10
Aboriginal	.02	.03
English spoken in the home	.59	.15
English as the mother tongue	.46	.15
Unemployed	.10	.03
No high school diploma	.30	.10
Postsecondary diploma	.44	.12
One-year mobility	.80	.05
Family income less than 30K	.32	.09

G4, and G7, class size and the proportion of children in special education were obtained from the Vancouver School District. For G4 and G7, the proportion of children at risk for reading and mathematics was obtained from the FSA. For K, the proportion of children at risk on the Language and Cognitive Development subscale was obtained from the EDI.

Analysis and Results

We conducted the analyses in the four successive steps described in the following paragraphs:

Phase I: Selection of Socioeconomic Indicators

It is not uncommon for independent variables (i.e., predictors) measuring similar constructs to be highly correlated with each other. A high correlation between predictors indicates that some of them can be strongly predicted by others, determining what is known as collinearity. Collinearity can become a problem in that it affects the way the beta coefficients of a regression model are estimated. Because we disposed of a number of related socioeconomic indicators, we conducted a test to check whether collinearity was present among our predictors. To do so, we used the computer software program SPSS 10.1 and produced a regression model in which all socioeconomic indicators were entered in one block to predict the proportion of highly competent K children. In the regression model, we selected the option for calculation of partial correlation and collinearity diagnostics. In collinearity diagnostics, researchers use two indexes to decide how much correlation between predictors is tolerable: Variance Inflation Factor (VIF) and Tolerance (obtained by dividing 1 by the VIF value). We considered as acceptable a correlation coefficient between predictors if it had a Tolerance equal to or larger than .05. According to that criterion, we decided to eliminate from the analyses the following three socioeconomic indicators: (a) percentage of immigrant population,

(b) percentage of population with English as primary language spoken at home, and (c) percentage of population with English as the mother tongue.

Phase II: Changes in Association Between Proportion of Highly Competent Children and Socioeconomic Indicators

In this phase of the analyses, we investigated the changes in the association between academic performance of highly competent children and neighborhood socioeconomic characteristics in K, G4, and G7.

To that end, we conducted three identical sets of linear regression procedures in which all socioeconomic indicators (see Table 1) were entered in one single block to predict the proportion of highly competent children. The difference between the three procedures was in the outcome variables: (a) proportion of highly competent K children, (b) proportion of highly competent G4 children, and (c) proportion of highly competent G7 children.

The results of the three procedures indicate that neighborhood socioeconomic indicators predicted only minimally the proportion of highly competent children in K, $R^2 = .120$, $F(8, 69) = 1.172$, $p = .329$. However, their predictive power increased sharply in G4, reading: $R^2 = .341$, $F(8, 69) = 4.462$, $p = .000$; numeracy: $R^2 = .352$, $F(8, 69) = 4.683$, $p = .000$, and again in G7, reading: $R^2 = .444$, $F(8, 62) = 6.199$, $p = .000$; numeracy: $R^2 = .380$, $F(8, 62) = 4.755$, $p = .000$. The trend for the increases was significant ($z = 2.75$, $p < .05$ for reading; $z = 2.22$, $p < .05$ for numeracy).

Phase III: Changes in Association Between Proportion of Highly Competent Children, Socioeconomic Indicators, and Class Composition

In this phase of the analysis, we investigated whether class composition changed the extent of the association between the proportion of highly competent children and the neighborhood socioeconomic indicators. We defined class composition as a combination of class size, proportion of children at risk, and proportion of children in special education. We entered those variables separately in the regression models so that we could investigate their differential contribution to the association between neighborhood socioeconomic indicators and proportion of highly competent children.

Thus, we conducted three identical sets of linear regression procedures in which the socioeconomic indicators were entered into the first block of the model, class size in the second block, proportion of children in special education in the third block, and proportion of children at risk in the fourth block.

Results of this analysis showed that multiple correlation squared (R^2) increased significantly only when the proportion of children at risk for reading and mathematics was added to the model. Class size and the proportion of children in special education did not increase the predictive power of neighborhood socioeconomic indicators, except in the case of G4 reading (see Table 2).

Table 2. Changes in R^2 Between Neighborhood Socioeconomic Status (SES) and Proportion of Highly Competent Children

R^2 Class	F R^2	Change	F	df	Change
EDI Language and Cognitive Scale					
Kindergarten					
1	.126	.126	1.139	71	1.139
2	.128	.001	1.007	71	.084
3	.129	.001	.901	71	.078
4	.152	.023	.975	71	1.621
Reading FSA					
Grade 4					
1	.355	.355	4.270	70	4.270*
2	.431	.076	5.143	70	8.170*
3	.431	.000	4.553	70	.000
4	.509	.077	5.551	70	9.263*
Grade 7					
1	.442	.442	5.550	64	5.550*
2	.444	.002	4.888	64	.215
3	.444	.000	4.320	64	.000
4	.573	.129	6.471	64	15.993*
Numeracy FSA					
Grade 4					
1	.358	.358	4.325	70	4.325*
2	.361	.003	3.824	70	.244
3	.375	.014	3.594	70	1.335
4	.480	.105	4.954	70	11.973*
Grade 7					
1	.380	.380	4.289	64	4.289*
2	.396	.016	4.003	64	1.445
3	.402	.006	3.628	64	.547
4	.603	.201	7.329	64	26.923*

Note. Class composition variables were added to R^2 = changes.

EDI = Early Development Instrument FSA = Foundation Skills Assessment; 1 = SES indicators; −2 = SES indicators + class size; 3 = SES indicators + class size + proportion of children in special education: 4 = SES indicators + class size + proportion of children in special education + proportion of children at risk for reading/numeracy difficulties.

*$p < .05$.

Phase IV: Changes in Association Between Proportion of Highly Competent Children, Socioeconomic Indicators, and Proportion of Children at Risk

Because class size and proportion of children in special education contributed negligibly to the previous model, we did not include them in this last phase of the analyses. Here we conducted the same analysis as in Phase I, but with the addition of proportion of children at risk to the model. That is, we conducted three sets of linear regression procedures in which all socioeconomic indicators and proportion of children at risk were entered into one single block to predict the proportion of highly competent children. Again, the difference between the three procedures was in the outcome variables, as reported in the previous phases.

As shown in Table 2, neighborhood socioeconomic indicators and proportion of children at risk for learning difficulties predicted only minimally the school proportion of highly competent children in K, $R^2 = .136$, $F(9, 68) = 1.186$, $p = .265$. However, their predictive power increased sharply in G4, reading: $R^2 = .443$, $F(9, 68) = 6.007$, $p = .001$; numeracy: $R^2 = .466$, $F(9, 68) = 6.591$, $p = .000$, and again in G7, reading: $R^2 = .584$, $F(8, 62) = 9.533$, $p = .000$; numeracy: $R^2 = .525$, $F(8, 62) = 9.604$, $p = .000$. The trend for these increases was significant ($z = 3.88$, $p < .001$ for reading and numeracy).

DISCUSSION

The results reported here show that, in kindergarten, the proportion of highly competent children was correlated weakly with neighborhood socioeconomic status (SES). In contrast, by Grade 4 the proportion of highly competent children, unlike high competence in kindergarten, was strongly socially patterned and more strongly correlated with neighborhood socioeconomic factors. Our analysis also has shown that the proportion of children at risk for difficulties in reading and mathematics was associated with the school proportion of highly competent children and that association became stronger in G4 and G7.

Why has this pattern emerged? Our analyses suggest that the proportion of vulnerable children entering school may be an important factor in that it is inversely (and strongly) associated with the proportion of children exceeding expectations in G4 and G7. Several possible explanations account for our findings. The first possibility is that highly competent children who live in lower socioeconomic neighborhoods are being held back by the academic pace that tends to characterize classrooms with large proportions of children who display difficulties in learning, regardless of the quality of instruction. A second possibility is that more qualified teachers may be attracted by higher socioeconomic schools and that they are better prepared to meet the special needs of highly competent children.

Conversely, as a third possibility, the effort needed to maintain an adequate pace of learning in the highly vulnerable classrooms may lead to teacher burnout that, in turn, leads to either (a) requests for school transfer by the highly motivated teachers or (b) a willingness by less motivated teachers to stay in the highly vulnerable schools and "go through the motions." Finally, because high vulnerability neighborhoods in Vancouver tend to be exceedingly multicultural in character, failure to effectively manage complex school-community relations may (a) adversely affect parent-teacher relations, (b) reduce classroom morale, and (c) slow the pace of learning in the classroom.

Each of the explanations for our findings likely contributes to some extent, but their implications for policy differ a great deal. To the extent that the second explanation applied, the emphasis would be taken off labor shortage and replaced with the quality of teaching necessary to eliminate perverse classroom composition effects in which vulnerable students decrease the academic pacing experienced by highly competent pupils. The focus would be on class size, level of teaching supervision, and provision for teacher aides. The issue at the intersection of the three explanations is teacher burnout in highly vulnerable classrooms and its long-term implications for academic pacing in schools in which high teacher burnout occurs. Perhaps it would be wise for highly motivated teachers to rotate through high burnout schools on, for example, a 3- to 5-year basis.

The final hypothesis regarding community-school relations places the response outside the specific classroom, into the realm of school leadership and community partnership. Because the policy implications diverge, one needs to understand the degree to which each explanation contributes or whether other explanations also contribute to our findings. By accessing information on teacher—school transfer patterns, variability over time in FSA tests in highly vulnerable schools, and case studies of community—school relations in highly vulnerable neighborhoods (currently underway), we hope to gain insights that will allow us in the near future to design a more rigorous analytic study of the contributions of the different explanations.

On a broader level, we addressed the issue of neighborhood socioeconomic mix. Literature already exists on the benefits to the early development of vulnerable children from living in mixed, rather than uniformly low, SES neighborhoods (Kaufman & Rosenbaum, 1992; Popkin, Rosenbaum, & Meaden, 1993; Rosenbaum, 1991; Rosenbaum & Popkin, 1991; Rosenbaum, Kulieke, & Rubinowitz, 1988). Our findings support and extend previous research indicating that schools located within low socioeconomic neighborhoods tend to concentrate vulnerable children. In a mixed neighborhood, one would expect that fewer vulnerable children enter school and that a reduced chance of a classroom pacing effect emerges. Whether a heterogeneous school district would gain net benefit from higher levels of neighborhood socioeconomic mixing would depend on whether the classroom pacing effect had a "tipping point."

As an example, consider two schools in a highly economically segregated community, in the affluent neighborhood (first community), 2% of the children are vulnerable in kindergarten compared with 20% of the children in a poor neighborhood (second community). Moreover, the 20% group of vulnerable children holds the highly competent children back, but the 2% group does not. In a better mixed community, the analogous proportions of vulnerable children might represent 9% of children in an affluent neighborhood and 13% of children in a poor neighborhood. If the relationship between the proportion of vulnerable children and classroom pacing is linear, the overall achievement levels in the two communities would be the same. If, however, the relationship is nonlinear, such that classroom pacing slows at a successively greater rate beyond a threshold proportion of vulnerable children, the second community would have higher academic achievement than would the first community. Such effects are within policy control through zoning regulations and through the distribution of nonmarket (social) housing throughout communities.

LIMITATIONS

Although our analysis has revealed some intriguing findings, it must be treated with caution. The data used here are serial cross-sectional and not longitudinal. Thus, the K, G4, and G7 children constitute three distinct groups. The validity of the analysis rests on the assumption that, nonetheless, children in a given school are comparable with one another over 8 years (K to G7, inclusive). That assumption could he undermined by (a) socioeconomically biased migrator effects, (b) sudden neighborhood socioeconomic changes from new housing developments, or (c) random year-to-year variations in the mixture of highly competent and vulnerable pupils. As a result of those limitations, it would be most useful for researchers to conduct a true prospective study, beginning with the Early Development Instrument in kindergarten and following children to at least Grade 7.

Stefania Maggi, The University of British Columbia; Clyde Hertzman, The University of British Columbia; Dafina Kohen, Statistics Canada and The University of British Columbia; Amedeo D'Angiulli, The University of British Columbia.

Address correspondence to Stefania Maggi, currently at The University College of The Cariboo, School of Education, Box 3010, 900 McGill Rd. Kamloops, British Columbia, Canada V2C 5N3 (E-mail: smaggi@cariboo.bc.ca)

CRITICAL THINKING QUESTIONS

1. In this article, the performance of highly competent children was inversely correlated with neighborhood socioeconomic status, and this effect became stronger with age. This suggests an increasing influence of nurture on performance. However, in the Plomin article, genetic influences appeared to grow stronger over time, suggesting increasing

influence of nature on performance. How can we reconcile these two findings?

2. What were the three possible alternatives Maggi et al. used to explain their findings? Discuss these, then take one of these explanations and describe how one would test it experimentally.

3. In this article, the authors investigated the performance of highly competent children via a cross-sectional design. What are the problems with utilizing this research design? Can we examine developmental change with a cross-sectional approach?

REFERENCES

Baydar, N., Brooks-Gunn, J., & Furstenberg, F. F., Jr. (1993). Early warning signs of functional illiteracy: Predictors in childhood and adolescence. *Child Development; 64*(3), 815–829.

Brooks-Gunn, J., Klebanov, P. K., Liaw, F., & Spiker, D. (1993). Enhancing the development of low birth weight premature infants: Changes in cognition and behavior over the first three years. *Child Development, 64*(3), 736–753.

Cappella, E., & Weinstein, R. S. (2001). Turning around reading achievement: Predictors of high school students' academic resilience. *Journal of Educational Psychology, 93*(4), 758–771.

Chase-Lansdale, P. L., & Gordon, R. L. (1996). Economic hardship and the development of 5- and 6-year-aids: Neighborhood and regional perspectives. *Child Development, 67*, 3338–3367.

Chase-Lansdale, L., Gordon, R., Brooks-Gunn, J., & Klebanov, E. K. (1997). Neighborhood and family influences on the intellectual and behavioral competence of preschool and early school-age children. In J. Brooks-Gann, G. J. Duncan, & J. L. Aber (Eds.), *Neighborhood poverty: Context and consequences for children* (pp. 79–118). New York: Sage.

D'Agostino, J. V. (2000). Instructional and school effects on students' longitudinal reading and mathematics achievements. *School Effectiveness and School Improvement, 11*(2), 197–235.

Darlington, R. B., Royce, J. M., Snipper, A. S., Murray, H. W., & Lazar, I. (1980). Preschool programs and later school competence of children from low-income families. *Science, 208*, 202–204.

Doherty, G. (1997). Zero to six: The basis for school readiness. (Report No. R-97-8-E). Ottawa, Ontario, Canada: Human Resources Development Canada, Applied Research Branch.

Duncan, G. J., & Brooks-Gunn J. (1997). *Consequences of growing up poor.* New York: Sage.

Haveman R., & Wolfe, B. (1995). The determinants of children's attainments: A review of methods and findings. *Journal of Economic Literature, 33,* 1829–1878.

Hertzman C. (1992). The lifelong impact of childhood experiences. *Daedalus, 123*(4), 167–180.

Hertzman C., McLean S., Kohen D., Dunn J., & Evans T. (2002). *Early Development in Vancouver: Report of the Community Asset Mapping Project (CAMP).* Ottawa, Ontario, Canada: Canadian Institute for Health Information.

Janus, M., & Offord, D. (2000) Reporting on readiness to learn at school in Canada. ISUMA: *Canadian Journal of Policy Research, 1*(2), 71–75.

Kaufman, J., & Rosenbaum, J. (1992). The education and employment of low-income black youth in white suburbs. *Educational Evaluation and Policy Analysis, 14*(3), 229–240.

Nye, B., Hedges, L. V., & Kostantopoulos, S. (2001). Are effects of small classes cumulative? Evidence from a Tennessee experiment. *The Journal of Educational Research, 94,* 336–345.

Padron, Y. N., Waxman, H. C., & Huang, S. L. (1999). Classroom behavior and learning environment differences between resilient and nonresilient elementary school students. *Journal of Education for Students Placed at Risk, 4*(1), 65–82.

Popkin, S., Rosenbaum, J., & Meaden, E. (1993). Labor market experiences of low-income black women in middle-class suburbs: Evidence from a survey of Gautreaux program participants. *Journal of Policy Analysis and Management, 12,* 556–573.

Power, C., & Hertzman, C. (1997). Social and biological pathways linking early life and adult disease. *British Medical Bulletin, 3,* 210–221.

Rosenbaum, J. E. (1991). Black pioneers: Do their moves to the suburbs increase economic opportunity for mothers and children? *Housing Policy Debate, 2*(4), 1179–1213.

Rosenbaum, J. E., Kulieke, M. J., & Ruhinowitz, L. S. (1988). White suburban schools' responses to low-income black children: Sources of successes and problems. *The Urban Review, 20*(1), 28–41.

Ross, D. P., & Roberts, E. (1999). *Income and child well-being: A new perspective on the poverty debate.* Ottawa, Canada: Canadian Council on Social Development.

U.S. National Educational Goals Panel. (1993). *Reconsidering children's early development and learning: Toward shared beliefs and vocabulary* (Report No. 9543). Washington, DC: Author.

11

Self and Personality

Shyness, Sadness, Curiosity, Joy: Is It Nature or Nurture?

Marc Peyser and Anne Underwood

Child Personality Development

Researchers have found that genes play a large role in shaping a child's emotional makeup, but a child's personality traits are also profoundly affected by his or her environment. Genetic and environmental factors combine in complex ways to shape a child's psychological development.

The wizards of genetics keep closing in on the biological roots of personality. It's not your imagination that one baby seems born cheerful and another morose. But that's not the complete picture. DNA is not destiny; experience plays a powerful role, too.

If any child seemed destined to grow up afraid of her shadow and just about anything else that moved, it was 2-year-old Marjorie. She was so painfully shy that she wouldn't talk to or look at a stranger. She was even afraid of friendly cats and dogs. When Jerome Kagan, a Harvard professor who discovered that shyness has a strong genetic component, sent a clown to play with Marjorie, she ran to her mother. "It was as if a cobra entered that room,"

Kagan says. His diagnosis: Marjorie showed every sign of inherited shyness, a condition in which the brain somehow sends out messages to avoid new experiences. But as Kagan continued to examine her over the years, Marjorie's temperament changed. When she started school, she gained confidence from ballet classes and her good grades, and she began to make friends. Her parents even coaxed her into taking horseback-riding lessons. Marjorie may have been born shy, but she has grown into a bubbly second grader.

For Marjorie, then, biology—more specifically, her genetic inheritance—was not her destiny. And therein lies our tale. In the last few years scientists have identified genes that appear to predict all sorts of emotional behavior, from happiness to aggressiveness to risk-taking. The age-old question of whether nature or nurture determines temperament seems finally to have been decided in favor of Mother Nature and her ever-deepening gene pool. But the answer may not be so simple after all. Scientists are beginning to discover that genetics and environment work together to determine personality as intricately as Astaire and Rogers danced. "If either Fred or Ginger moves too fast, they both stumble," says Stanley Greenspan, a pediatric psychiatrist at George Washington University and the author of "The Growth of the Mind." "Nature affects nurture affects nature and back and forth. Each step influences the next." Many scientists now believe that some experiences can actually alter the structure of the brain. An aggressive toddler, under the right circumstances, can essentially be rewired to channel his energy more constructively. Marjorie can overcome her shyness—forever. No child need be held captive to her genetic blueprint. The implications for child rearing—and social policy—are profound.

While Gregor Mendel's pea plants did wonders to explain how humans inherit blue eyes or a bald spot, they turn out to be an inferior model for analyzing something as complex as the brain. The human body contains about 100,000 genes, of which 50,000 to 70,000 are involved in brain function. Genes control the brain's neurotransmitters and receptors, which deliver and accept mental messages like so many cars headed for their assigned parking spaces. But there are billions of roads to each parking lot, and those paths are highly susceptible to environmental factors. In his book "The New View of Self," Dr. Larry Siever, a psychiatry professor at Mount Sinai Medical Center, writes about how the trauma of the Holocaust caused such intense gene fir: scrambling in some survivors that their children inherited the same stress-related abnormalities. "Perhaps the sense of danger and uncertainty associated with living through such a time is passed on in the family milieu and primes the biological systems of the children as well," says Siever. He added that that might explain why pianist David Helfgott, the subject of the movie "Shine," had his mental breakdown.

A gene is only a probability for a given trait, not a guarantee. For that trait to be expressed, a gene often must be "turned on" by an outside force before it does its job. High levels of stress apparently activate a variety of genes, including those suspected of being involved in fear, shyness and some mental illnesses. Children conceived during a three-month famine in the Netherlands during a Nazi blockade in 1945 were later found to have twice the rate of schizophrenia as did Dutch children born to parents who were spared the trauma of famine. "Twenty years ago, you couldn't get your research funded if you were looking for a genetic basis for schizophrenia, because everyone knew it was what your mother did to you in the first few years of life, as Freud said," says Robert Plomin, a geneticist at London's Institute of Psychiatry. "Now you can't get funded unless you're looking for a genetic basis. Neither extreme is right, and the data show why. There's only a 50 percent concordance between genetics and the development of schizophrenia."

Scientists have been devoting enormous energy to determining what part of a given character trait is "heritable" and what part is the result of socialization. Frank Sulloway's book "Born to Rebel," which analyzes the influence of birth order on personality, opened a huge window on a universal—and largely overlooked—environmental factor. But that's a broad brushstroke. Most studies focus on remarkably precise slivers of human emotions. One study at Allegheny University in Pennsylvania found that the tendency for a person to throw dishes or slam doors when he's angry is 40 percent heritable, while the likelihood a person will yell in anger is only 28 percent heritable. The most common method for determining these statistics is studying twins. If identical twins are more alike in some way than are fraternal twins, that trait is believed to have a higher likelihood of being inherited. But the nature-nurture knot is far from being untied.

The trick, then, is to isolate a given gene and study the different ways environment interacts with it. For instance, scientists believe that people with the longer variety of a dopamine-4 receptor gene are biologically predisposed to be thrill seekers. Because the gene appears to make them less sensitive to pain and physical sensation, the children are more likely to, say, crash their tricycles into a wall, just to see what it feels like. "These are the daredevils," says Greenspan. But they need not be. Given strict boundaries, Greenspan says, thrill-seeking kids can be taught to modulate and channel their overactive curiosity. A risk-taking child who likes to pound his fist into hard objects can be taught games that involve hitting softly as well. "If you give them constructive ways to meet their needs," says Greenspan, "they can become charismatic, action-oriented leaders."

Shyness has been studied perhaps more than any other personality trait. Kagan, who has monitored 500 children for more than 17 years at Harvard, can detect telltale signs of shyness in babies even before they're born. He's found that the hearts of shy children in the womb consistently beat faster than 140 times a minute, which is much faster than the heartbeats of other babies. The shy fetus is already highly reactive, wired to overmonitor his environment. But he can also outgrow this predisposition if his parents gently but firmly desensitize him to the situations that cause anxiety, such as encouraging him to play with other children or, as in Marjorie's fear of animals, taking her to the stables and teaching her to ride a horse. Kagan has found that by the age of 4, no more than 20 percent of the previously shy children remain that way.

Will the reprogramming last into adulthood? Because evidence of the role of genes has been discovered only recently, it's still too early to tell. But studies of animals give some indication. Stephen Suomi at the National Institute of Child Health and Human Development works with rhesus monkeys that possess the same genetic predisposition to shyness that affects humans. He's shown that by giving a shy monkey to a foster mother who is an expert caregiver, the baby will outgrow the shyness. Even more surprising, the once shy monkey will become a leader among her peers and an unusually competent parent, just like the foster mom. Though she will likely pass along her shyness genes to her own child, she will teach it how to overcome her predisposition, just as she was taught. And the cycle continues—generations of genetically shy monkeys become not just normal, but superior, adults and parents. The lesson, says Suomi: "You can't prejudge anyone at birth. No matter what your genetic background, a negative characteristic you're born with may even turn out to be an advantage."

But parents aren't scientists, and it's not always easy to see how experience can influence a child's character. A baby who smiles a lot and makes eye contact is, in part, determining her own environment, which in turn affects her temperament. As her parents coo and smile and wrinkle their noses in delighted response, they are reinforcing their baby's sunny disposition. But what about children who are born with low muscle tone, who at 4 months can barely hold up their own heads, let alone smile? Greenspan has discovered that mothers of these kids smile at the baby for a while, but when the affection isn't returned, they give up. And so does the baby, who over time fails to develop the ability to socialize normally. "If you move in the wrong patterns, the problem is exacerbated," Greenspan says. He has found that if parents respond to nonsmiling babies by being superanimated—like Bob Barker hosting a game show—they can engage their child's interest in the world.

The ramifications of these findings clearly have the potential to revolutionize child-rearing theory and practice. But to an uncertain end. "Our society has a strong belief that what happens in childhood determines your fate. If you have a happy childhood, everything will be all right. That's silly," says Michael Lewis, director of the Institute for the Study of Child Development in New Jersey and the author of "Altering Fate." Lewis estimates that experience ultimately rewrites 90 percent of a child's personality traits, leaving an adult with only one tenth of his inborn temperament. "The idea that early childhood is such a powerful moment to see individual differences in biology or environment is not valid," he says. "We are too open to and modifiable by experience." Some scientists warn that attempting to reprogram even a narrow sliver of childhood emotions can prove to be a daunting task, despite research's fascinating new insights. "Children are not a 24-hour controlled experiment," says C. Robert Cloninger, a professor of psychiatry and genetics at the Washington University School of Medicine in St. Louis. "If you put a child in a Skinner box, then maybe you could have substantial influence." So, mindful of the blinding insights of geneticists and grateful for the lingering influences of environment, parents must get on with the business of raising their child, an inexact science if ever there was one.

CRITICAL THINKING QUESTIONS

1. Our genes are the product of evolutionary pressures making some variants more likely in succeeding generations. However, according to this article, substantial change in the phenotype is possible when the right combination of environmental factors is met. Why would evolution fashion a system so amenable to environmental influences? What would be the advantage?

2. Peyser and Underwood describe how mothers with children of low muscle tone initially attempt to engage their child, but tend to give up in the face of an unresponsive infant. Consequently, over time, the infant is then deprived of many socialization influences. Essentially, the initial predisposition of the infant interacts with the caregiving environment and "snowballs" to make matters worse. Pick a temperamental or physical characteristic and describe how parental influences might serve to exacerbate initial tendencies in the same manner.

12

Gender Roles and Sexuality

Differences in Finger Length Ratios Between Self-Identified "Butch" and "Femme" Lesbians

Windy M. Brown (1), Christopher J. Finn (1), Bradley M. Cooke (1), and S. Marc Breedlove (2, 3)

There is indirect evidence that heightened exposure to early androgen may increase the probability that a girl will develop a homosexual orientation in adulthood. One such putative marker of early androgen exposure is the ratio of the length of the index finger (2D) to the ring finger (4D), which is smaller in male humans than in females, and is smaller in lesbians than in heterosexual women. Yet there is also evidence that women may have different sexual orientations at different times in their lives, which suggests that other influences on female sexual orientation, presumably social, are at work as well. We surveyed individuals from a gay pride street fair and found that lesbians who identified themselves as "butch" had a significantly smaller 2D:4D than did those who identified themselves as "femme." We conclude that increased early androgen exposure plays a role in only some cases of female homosexuality, and that the sexual orientation of "femme" lesbians is unlikely to have been influenced by early androgens.

Archives of Sexual Behavior, Feb 2002, v31 i1 p123(5).

"Differences in Finger Length Ratios Between Self-Identified "Butch" and "Femme" Lesbians" by Windy M. Brown, Christopher J. Finn, Bradley M. Cooke, and S. Marc Breedlove. © 2002 Plenum Publishing Corporation.

n nonhuman mammals, sexual differentiation of behavior seems largely driven by exposure to steroid hormones during the perinatal period (Breedlove, Cooke, & Jordan, 1998). The Y chromosome in males causes the undifferentiated gonads to develop as testes, and the testes to secrete androgen, which masculinizes the structure of the brain, permanently molding the animal's behavior to a male-like form (Phoenix, Goy, Gerall, & Young, 1959). Whether early androgen exposure also directly alters the structure of the developing human brain, and thereby adult behavior, remains undetermined.

In the study of sexual orientation, there is little direct evidence that individual differences in early androgen exposure affect the sexual preferences of men. In women, however, there have been several reports of a difference between heterosexual and homosexual women in purported markers of prenatal or neonatal androgen exposure. McFadden and Champlin (2000) found that auditory evoked potentials (AEP) are more masculine in lesbians than in heterosexual women. Because the sex difference in AEP is present in newborn humans, and because other somatic sex differences in newborns appear to be due to the masculinizing influence of androgen in males, presumably AEP are influenced by, and can therefore serve as markers for, fetal androgen exposure. Thus the AEP results suggest that homosexual women were exposed to more fetal androgen than were heterosexual women. McFadden and Champlin also found that the AEP of homosexual men suggested that they, if anything, had experienced significantly higher levels of perinatal androgen than did heterosexual men. McFadden and Pasanen (1998) also found that otoacoustic emissions, which are also sexually dimorphic at birth (and therefore may also serve as markers for fetal androgen), are significantly more male-like in homosexual women than in heterosexual women. This result is a further indication that lesbians may have been exposed to higher fetal androgen levels than heterosexual women (for an overview, see McFadden, 2002).

Another purported somatic marker of fetal androgen is the ratio of the length of the index finger (2D) to the ring finger (4D). This ratio, 2D:4D, is smaller in men than in women (Ecker, 1875), a sex difference that is stable from 2 years of age to adulthood (Manning, Scott, Wilson, & Lewis-Jones, 1998). As most somatic differences between young boys and girls have been attributed to differences in exposure to androgen before and just after birth (George & Wilson, 1994), the sex difference in 2D:4D was presumed to reflect sex differences in early androgen.

We have tested this hypothesis by examining the 2D:4D of people with congenital adrenal hyperplasia (CAH). CAH is a disorder that causes the adrenals to produce excessive androgens beginning prenatally and extending to treatment, which usually begins shortly after birth following an accurate diagnosis. We found that the ratios were indeed smaller in CAH females than in control females, and were also smaller in CAH males than in control males (Brown, Hines, Fane, & Breedlove, 2001). The difference between CAH males and control males was especially prominent when comparing relatives, suggesting that genetic background can affect the finger length ratios but that, within a particular genetic background, greater early androgen exposure reduces the finger ratios. We have also found a similar sex difference in the digit length ratios of mice: rear paw 2D:4D is smaller in males than in females at weaning and in adulthood (Brown, Finn, & Breedlove, 2001), which suggests that adult digit length ratios may provide a retrospective indication of perinatal androgens in many mammalian species.

Accordingly, the report of Williams et al. (2000) that the 2D:4D of homosexual women was more masculine (smaller) than that of heterosexual women indicates again that lesbians are, on average, exposed to more prenatal androgen than are heterosexual women. If so, then increased exposure to fetal androgen may increase the probability of homosexuality in human females. This study found no differences in the 2D:4D of heterosexual versus homosexual men.

If early hormone levels affect human sexual orientation in the same manner as they do other sex dimorphic behaviors in other animals, this influence would be expected to be organizational in nature such that the behavior pattern affected is set from a young age and remains constant throughout the life span. There is some evidence, however, that some women have a heterosexual orientation during certain periods of their lives and a homosexual orientation at other periods (Diamond, 1998). This suggests that other factors, including social influences, can also affect sexual orientation in women. Therefore, presumably some of the lesbians studied in the previously cited reports were exposed to low levels of androgen in development, i.e., perinatal androgens played no role in the development of their sexual orientation. Because other, nonandrogenic factors influence female sexual orientation, the experimental detection of effects of early androgen, especially via indirect measures, requires large sample sizes. We therefore wondered whether it would be possible to subdivide lesbian participants into groups in which perinatal androgen exposure might be more or less likely to have played a role in the development of a homosexual orientation. Because some lesbians consider themselves to be more masculine ("butch") than other women, we tested whether the finger length ratios of "butch" lesbians would show evidence of greater perinatal androgen exposure than those of "femme" lesbians.

METHODS

A booth was rented for the August 2000 Gay Pride Mardi Gras in Oakland, CA. All adult participants were offered a California Lottery "scratcher" ticket in return for answering an anonymous survey that asked their age, sex at birth, and number of older brothers and sisters.

Participants and Measures. Participants identified themselves as "exclusively heterosexual," "predominantly heterosexual," "bisexual," "predominantly homosexual," or "exclusively homosexual." They were also asked the gender of their sexual partners ("exclusively males," "predominantly males," "males and females equally," "predominantly females," or "exclusively females") and the gender of sexual partners in their fantasies. These latter two questions were asked to confirm self-reports of orientation and, in this study, all participants gave answers that were consistent with their reported sexual orientation. They were also asked to answer the following question: "If I had to describe myself as one of the two types below, I would consider my overall outlook to be (circle one)": with the choices butch and femme on the line beneath. The questionnaire informed them that answering any question was voluntary and would not affect their receipt of a ticket. Participants were not asked to report their ethnicity.

The participants then had their hands copied on a portable photocopier. A clear plexiglass form was placed on the glass platen. This form had two posts, 6mm in diameter, 147 mm apart. Participants were asked to place their hands flat, palm-down, thumbs near each other, fingers on each hand together, on the form with the posts between the index and middle fingers of each hand, snug against the junction of the two fingers. A millimeter scale was present 12 mm lateral to the posts and the participants' middle fingers were aligned on this scale. A white plastic bag, filled with rice for ballast, was placed over the hands before photocopying. Matching numbered stickers were affixed to the back of each questionnaire and photocopy to discern which answers were associated with each photocopy.

Finger lengths were measured by an experimenter, without knowledge of any participant's group membership. If the tip of either finger was obscured in the photocopy, then no ratio was available for that hand for that participant. Measures were taken for each finger to the nearest 0.5 mm, based on their alignment to the photocopied ruler running along the middle finger. This method of measuring finger length differs slightly from other recent reports, but is much more efficient than the method we used previously (Williams et al., 2000). It also more closely matches the measurement method reported by George (1930), confirming Ecker's report (Ecker, 1875). Two mixed-design ANOVAs, with an independent factor of either male/female (to evaluate sex differences) or butch/femme (to evaluate lesbian subgroups), and right and left hand finger ratios as repeated measures, were conducted. Further analysis of differences between groups were evaluated by Student's t tests, with all reported p values two-tailed.

RESULTS

The present measurement method detected the previously reported sex difference in 2D:4D between the 267 female and 168 male participants. ANOVA revealed a sex difference in which ratios were greater in females than in males, $F(1, 432) = 28.3$, $p < .001$, a laterality effect in which the ratios were greater on the right than on the left, $F(1, 432) = 6.0$, $p < .02$, and a significant interaction of the two factors, $F(1, 432) = 18.6$, $p < .001$. Student's tests indicated that the interaction was due to a greater sex difference on the right than on the left. For the right hand, the ratio was 0.994 ± 0.003 (SEM) for women, 0.958 ± 0.004 for men, $t(431) = 6.6$, $p < 10^{-10}$); for the left hand, the ratio was 0.967 ± 0.003 for women and 0.938 ± 0.004 for men, $t(431) = 5.9$, $p < 10^8$. Our previous report (Williams et al., 2000) also found the sex difference in 2D:4D to be greater on the right hand than on the left hand.

Of the 267 women, 29 identified themselves as heterosexual (either "predominantly heterosexual" or "exclusively heterosexual"), 28 as bisexual, 207 as homosexual (either "predominantly homosexual" or "exclusively homosexual"), and one declined to answer the questions about sexual orientation. The data from bisexuals were not examined. Among the homosexual women, 89 identified themselves as femme, 87 as butch, whereas 31 declined to answer the question. Self-identified butch versus femme lesbians were not significantly different in age (femme: mean of 39.41 ± .98 years, range, 22–58; butch: 41.12 ± .90 years, range, 24–66).

ANOVA revealed that the 2D:4D of lesbians were lateralized, as the ratio was greater on the right than on the left, $F(1, 173)$ 55.5, $p < .001$. The ratios of butch lesbians were smaller than those of femme lesbians, although the difference was only marginally significant, $F(1, 173) = 3.75$, $p = .056$. The interaction between lesbian subtype and laterality was not significant, $F(1, 173) = 1.02$, $p > .30$, but t-tests indicated that the difference between butch and femme lesbians was greater on the right hand than on the left (Fig. 1) [Figure Omitted]. (All figures referenced can be found within the online version of this article, at http://www.infotrac-college.com.)

The right hand 2D:4D of butch lesbians (0.985 ± 0.005) was smaller than that of femme lesbians (1.00 ± 0.006), $t(174) = 2.15$, $p = .033$. The difference between the two groups of lesbians on the right hand ratio seemed to be due entirely to differences in the length of the ring finger (femme: 666.3 ± 5.12 mm; butch: 683.3 ± 5.24), $t(174) = 2.33$, $p = .02$. The length of the index finger did not differ between the two groups on either hand (femme: left 673.4 ± 5.03, right 667.5 ± 5.77; butch: left 678.2 ± 4.98, right 672.5 ± 5.31; ps > .50), which suggests that the two groups did not differ in overall body size. Differences between butch and femme lesbians in the length of the ring finger on the left hand did not reach significance (femme: 692.1 ± 4.87; butch: 704.4 ± 4.97), $t(174) = 1.76$, $p = .08$ (two-tailed). Therefore the 2D:4D ratio did not differ significantly between the two groups on the left hand (butch: 0.964 ± 0.004; femme: 0.974 ± 0.005).

DISCUSSION

We found that it was possible to classify homosexual women into two self-reported categories: those who regard themselves as having a "butch" outlook and those who regard themselves as having a "femme" outlook. Although there is debate over the validity of segregating homosexual women into these categories (Laner & Laner, 1980), most participants in this study appeared to intuitively understand what we were referring to by these classifications and most of them, when asked, appeared to readily identify more with one than the other. These two groups differed significantly in the 2D:4D ratio of the right hand, suggesting that the femme group had been exposed to less prenatal androgen than had the butch group. Nevertheless, the overlap between the two groups for this measure was considerable. The data thus indicate that there are more factors influencing sexual orientation than simply early androgen exposure.

The finding that women who identify themselves as either butch or femme lesbians differ in this biological marker for androgen suggests that it may be worthwhile to try to more rigorously define subgroups of individuals regarded as either heterosexual or homosexual. The present classification was simple (an answer to a single, rather amorphous question) and therefore surely crude. It should be possible, with more extensive probing of personality traits, to more accurately classify homosexual women. Such refined classifications might reveal a greater difference in 2D:4D, or might reveal personality traits that covary with finger ratios, which might shed light on the butch—femme distinction. For example, after conducting the study we learned of the report by Wilson (1983) regarding women who answered a newspaper survey. Those who reported that their index finger was shorter than their ring finger were more likely to describe themselves as "assertive and competitive" than those whose index finger was longer than the ring finger. Again, the sample size was large (985 women), so it is not a question of whether early androgens determine this personality style, only whether they increase the probability of such a personality developing. It is possible that the present differences in 2D:4D reflect a difference in assertiveness between butch and femme lesbians.

The 2D:4D difference between butch and femme lesbians is consistent with the idea that early androgens have some influence on later sexual orientation, at least in females. The present findings also conform to the report from Singh, Vidaurri, Zambarano, and Dabbs (1999) that butch lesbians had a higher waist-to-hip ratio, higher salivary testosterone levels, and more reports of childhood gender-atypical behavior than did femme lesbians. These results and the previously discussed auditory system measures suggest that early exposure to androgen can increase the probability of a homosexual orientation in human females.

We have so far detected no difference between heterosexual and homosexual men in 2D:4D, suggesting that early androgens do not differ between the two groups and may not play a role in the development of male sexual orientation. But the present findings suggest that it might be possible to classify homosexual men into categories that might reveal a difference in early androgen exposure. For example, some homosexual men report a history of gender nonconformity as children, whereas others do not. It is possible that a relative lack of early androgen exposure might contribute to the development of homosexuality in the former, and/or that a relative surplus of early androgen might contribute to homosexuality in the latter. Robinson and Manning

(2000) in fact report that the finger ratios of gay men differ according their score on the Kinsey sexual orientation scale.

We have several times found the sex difference in 2D:4D to be greater on the right hand than on the left (Williams et al., 2000, the present study, and unpublished observations), as have other groups (Manning et al., 1998). We also found that the difference between CAH and control women was greater on the right hand than on the left (Brown, Hines, et al., 2001). These data suggest that the right hand finger ratios are more sensitive to prenatal androgen than are those on the left. We can offer no explanation for why androgen would affect the developing right hand more than the left.

While reviewing the proofs for this article, we learned that Tortorice (2001) recently reported 2D:4D to be smaller in self-rated butch lesbians than in femme lesbians.

(1) Department of Psychology, University of California, Berkeley, California. (2) Neuroscience Program, Michigan State University, East Lansing, Michigan. (3) To whom correspondence should be addressed at Department of Neuroscience, Psychology Research Building, Michigan State University, East Lansing, Michigan 48824; e-mail: breedsm@msu.edu.

ACKNOWLEDGEMENTS

Supported by NIH Grant MH58703, and and NSERC fellowship to WMB.

Received August 7, 2001; revision received September 4, 2001; accepted September 4, 2001.

CRITICAL THINKING QUESTIONS

1. In the Brown et al. study, the researchers found that the 2D:4D ratio on the right hand was significantly correlated with "butch" or "femme" orientation in lesbians, but no such relationship existed for males. Does this suggest that prenatal hormonal environments are more important in females than males? Why or why not?

2. Brown et al. cite research indicating that women with a more masculinized 2D:4D ratio more commonly describe themselves as "assertive and competitive" than those with a more feminized ratio. What does this finding imply about potential biological differences in male and female assertiveness and competitiveness? Discuss the interaction between the potential biological influences on these traits and how society might serve to exacerbate or minimize these differences.

3. Whether or not homosexuality is the result of biology or environment is a contentious political debate that colors the related ethical issues. Discuss

whether or not the nature/nurture distinction should be addressed in political decisions regarding same-sex marriage.

REFERENCES

Bailey, J. M., Pillard, R. C., Neale, M. C., & Agyei, Y. (1993). Heritable factors influence sexual orientation in women. *Archives of General Psychiatry, 50,* 217–223.

Breedlove, S. M., Cooke, B., & Jordan, C. L. (1998). The orthodox view of sexual differentiation of the brain. *Brain, Behavior and Evolution, 54,* 8–14.

Brown, W. M., Finn, C., & Breedlove, S. M. (2001). A sex difference in the digit length ratio in mice (Abstract). *Hormones and Behavior, 39,* 325.

Brown, W. M., Hines, M., Fane, B., & Breedlove, S. M. (2001). Masculinized finger length ratios in humans with congenital adrenal hyperplasia (CAH) (Abstract). *Hormones and Behavior, 39,* 325–326.

Diamond, L. M. (1998). Development of sexual orientation among adolescent and young adult women. *Developmental Psychology, 34,* 1085–1095.

Ecker, A. (1875). Einige bemerkungen uben einen schwankenden charakter in der hand des menschen. [Some remarks about a varying character in the hand of humans.] *Archiv fur Anthropologie, 8,* 68–74.

George, F. W., & Wilson, J. D. (1994). Sex determination and differentiation. In E. Knobil & J. D. Neil (Eds.), *The physiology of reproduction* (pp. 3–28). New York: Raven Press.

George, R. (1930). Human finger types. Anatomical Record, 46, 199–204.

Laner, M. R., & Laner, R. H. (1980). Sexual preference or personal style? Why lesbians are disliked. *Journal of Homosexuality, 5,* 339–356.

Manning, J. T., Scott, D., Wilson, J., & Lewis-Jones, D. I. (1998). The ratio of 2nd to 4th digit length: A predictor of sperm numbers and concentrations of testosterone, luteinizing hormone and oestrogen. *Human Reproduction, 13,* 3000–3004.

McFadden, D. (2002). Masculinization effects in the auditory system. *Archives of Sexual Behavior, 31,* 93–105.

McFadden, D., & Champlin, C. A. (2000). Comparison of auditory evoked potentials in heterosexual, homosexual, and bisexual males and females. *Journal of the Association of Research in Otolaryngology, 1,* 89–99.

McFadden, D., & Pasanen, E.G. (1998). Comparison of the auditory systems of heterosexuals and homosexuals: Click-evoked otoacoustic emissions. Proceedings of the National Academy of Sciences of the United States of America, 95, 2709–2713.

Phoenix, C. H., Goy, R. W., Gerall A. A., & Young, W. C. (1959), Organizing action of prenatally administered testosterone propionate on the tissues mediating mating behavior in the female guinea pig. *Endocrinology, 65,* 369–382.

Robinson, S. J., & Manning, J. T. (2000). The ratio of 2nd to 4th digit length and male homosexuality. *Evolution and Human Behavior, 21,* 333–345.

Singh, D., Vidaurri, M., Zambarano, R. J., & Dabbs, J. M. (1999). Lesbian erotic role identification: Behavioral, morphological, and hormonal correlates. *Journal of Personality and Social Psychology, 76,* 1035–1049.

Tortorice, J. (2001). Gender identity, sexual orientation, and second-to-fourth digit ratio in females [abstract]. *Human Behavior and Evolution Society Abstracts, 13,* 35.

Williams, T. J., Pepitone, M. E., Christensen, S. E., Cooke, B. M., Huberman, A. D., Breedlove, T. J., Jordan, C. L., et al. (2000). Finger length patterns indicate an influence of fetal androgens on human sexual orientation. *Nature, 404,* 455–456.

Wilson, G. D. (1983). Finger-length as an index of assertiveness in women. *Personality and Individual Differences, 4,* 111–112.

13

Social Cognition and Moral Development

Children's Use of Gaze and Limb Movement Cues to Infer Deception

Ken J. Rotenberg and Carey Sullivan

A sample of 96 children from kindergarten, 2nd, 4th, and 6th grades judged the truthfulness of peers who varied in gaze and limb movement while providing verbal communications. Results indicated that children attributed greater lying to the peers who displayed indirect rather than direct gaze and active rather than non-active limb movement. The use of these cues was more evident in 4th- and 6th-grade children than it was in kindergarten and 2nd-grade children. Pilot studies indicated that adults and children as young as 5–6 years of age associated indirect gaze and active limb movement with anxiety. The findings are discussed with respect to children's theory of mind, concepts of lying, understanding of display rules, and learning of physiological cues associated with deception.

Researchers have been interested in the types of cues that individuals use to infer whether others are deceiving (see DePaulo, Stone, & Lassiter, 1985). There is evidence to suggest that adults believe that a person

Journal of Genetic Psychology, June 2003, v164 i2 p175(13).

experiences arousal and anxiety when attempting to deceive and, moreover, he or she will reveal that by a corresponding set of cues (Kraut, 1978; Riggio & Friedman, 1983; Vrij, Edward, & Bull, 2001; Vrij & Semin, 1996). For example, adults have been found to infer deception from cues associated with anxiety, such as indirect rather than direct gaze, active rather than nonactive postural shifts or limb movements, and high rather than low vocal pitch (Buller & Aune, 1987; Zuckerman, Koestner, & Driver, 1981). According to meta-analyses and some narrative analyses of research, there is a weak relation between those cues and the cues that reveal actual deception in adults. Although high vocal pitch has been found to be associated with actual deception, indirect gaze and active limb movements have not been found to be associated with deception (DePaulo, 1992; Vrij et al., 2001; Vrij & Semin, 1996; Zuckerman, DePaulo, & Rosenthal, 1981).

In contrast to the research on adults, there are not many studies on children's use of cues associated with anxiety to infer deception. The present study was designed to fill that gap in our knowledge by examining whether, and if so at what age, children infer deception from cues associated with anxiety, notably indirect gaze and active limb movement. There are several lines of research in developmental psychology that are related to that issue: theory of mind, concepts of lying, display rules, and learning of physiological cues revealing deception. The lines of research differ in the mechanisms responsible for children's use of cues associated with anxiety. According to the learning of the physiological cues for deception account, children learn that certain cues are indicative of anxiety and thus, presumably, of deception. The other lines of research are based on the assumption that children cognitively appraise the person displaying the cues by assessing his or her intentions to deceive, strategies for hiding deception, or emotional states associated with deception.

THEORY OF MIND

Children's understanding of deception has been examined in research on the development of the theory of mind. Researchers have investigated whether children engage in deception or understand the act of deception as a means of determining whether children are able to conceptualize that people can hold false beliefs. Researchers have indicated that children demonstrate that ability at least by the end of the preschool period (5 years of age; Chandler, Fritz, & Hala, 1989; Davis, 2001; Flavell, 2000; Ruffman, Olson, Ash, & Keenan, 1993). Some researchers indicated that some facets of theory of mind continue to develop across middle childhood, specifically the ability to understand that a person's mind is an interpretive, constructive processor (i.e., Carpendale & Chandler, 1996).

Children's theory of mind abilities could foster their use of cues associated with anxiety to infer deception. Children may be prone to use such cues if they believe that the person displaying them is attempting to create a false belief in others—the belief that he or she is stating the truth. The theory of mind research implies that children may be able to use cues associated with anxiety to infer deception by the age of 5. The theory of mind research does not, however, yield specific predictions about (a) whether children will use such cues and, if so, (b) when in the course of development they will show that pattern of judgment.

CONCEPTS OF LYING

Piaget (1965) hypothesized that young children do not base their concepts of lying on the intention to deceive but that they gradually acquire that conceptualization of lying over the 6- to 10-year-old age span. The findings of a number of studies provide some support for Piaget's hypothesis (Peterson, Peterson, & Seeto, 1983; Wimmer, Gruber, & Pemer, 1984). Some studies, however, have qualified and extended Piaget's hypothesis. For example, Bussey (1992) found that young children (4–5 years old) believed that lying is more morally reprehensible than telling the truth. Also, her study indicated that only elementary-school-age children believed that a person who lies experiences more negative evaluative reactions (e.g., feels guilty) than does a person who tells the truth. This information is relevant to the present issue. Children's understanding that lying involves the intention to deceive could foster their use of the cues associated with anxiety to infer deception. Furthermore, children's use of those cues may be facilitated if they believe that a person feels guilty when lying; guilt presumably produces anxiety that would be potentially shown by cues such as indirect gaze and active limb movement. On the basis of this line of research, children's use of the cues associated with anxiety to infer deception would be expected to increase across the 6- to 10-year-old age span (middle childhood).

UNDERSTANDING DISPLAY RULES

Researchers have found that young children (4-year-olds) distinguish between an individual's expression of emotion and his or her display of that emotion (Gardner, Harris, Ohmoto, & Hamazaki, 1988; Harris, Donnelly, Guz, & Pitt-Watson, 1986). Research on display rules indicates, though, that children's knowledge of the social rules prescribing the social conditions guiding individuals' expression of emotions increases across the 4- to 10-year-old age span (Gnepp & Hess, 1986; Joshi & MacLean, 1994; Saarni, 1979). The use of anxiety cues reflects an understanding of a display rule; the rule prescribes that a person who lies experiences anxiety and reveals that emotional state by displaying a given set of behavioral cues (the anxiety cue display rule).

Researchers have indicated that family experiences contribute to children's understanding of display rules (Jones, Abbey, & Cumberland, 1998), and it is possible that the anxiety cue display rule is acquired by direct socialization practices (Saarni & Salisch, 1993) in which parents verbally convey that rule to their children.

LEARNING PHYSIOLOGICAL CUES
FOR DECEPTION

There is evidence that deception is associated with anxiety as revealed by physiological changes, such as increases in the galvanic skin response and accelerated heart rate (e.g., Goedert, Rill, & Gerhard, 2001). As initially reported, however, researchers have indicated that cues that are thought to be associated with anxiety, such as indirect gaze and active limb movements, are not associated with deception. Similar findings have been obtained with children. For example, in a study by Lewis, Stanger, and Sullivan (1989), 3-year-old children either complied with the experimenter's instructions not to peek at a toy or they peeked at the toy despite those instructions. Subsequently, when the experimenter asked the children about their behavior, they admitted (told the truth) or denied (deceived) their transgression. Later, observers coded the children's facial and body reactions, and 60 adults judged the truthfulness of the children's responses from videotapes.

Lewis et al. (1989) found that children did not display different facial and body cues when deceiving than when they were telling the truth; that sameness in facial and body cues included gaze aversion and nervous touching. Also, the adults could not distinguish between children who deceived as opposed to those who were telling the truth. Lewis (1993) reported other studies demonstrating similar patterns in children ranging from 3 to 6 years of age. These findings weigh against the idea that children learn physiological cues associated with anxiety and use them to infer deception. If children and adults do not display greater indirect gaze and limb movements when deceiving than when telling the truth, then children cannot directly learn that those cues are associated with deception.

CHILDREN'S USE OF CUES TO
INFER DECEPTION

Researchers have examined the types of cues that children use to infer deception. This past research has focused on children's use of discrepancy cues (Bugental, Kaswan, & Love, 1970; Friedman, 1979; Rotenberg, Simourd, & Moore, 1989) and valence of cues (DePaulo, Jordan, Irvine, & Laser, 1982;

Rotenberg et al.). To our knowledge, only Rotenberg's (1991) study addressed whether children use cues associated with anxiety to infer deception. In his study, second-, fourth-, and sixth-grade children were presented statements allegedly made by a peer regarding their preferences (e.g., "I like that food," "I do not like that shirt"). The children were asked how they would decide whether the peer was lying rather than telling the truth and what cues that would lead them to draw that conclusion. Rotenberg found that the children frequently identified the cues associated with anxiety for deception, notably limb movements and gaze. The identification of those cues tended to increase with age in a linear fashion. Rotenberg's study is limited because (a) children evaluated hypothetical events and (b) conclusions about children's use of the cues depended on the adults' (coders') interpretation of the children's verbal reports.

GENDER DIFFERENCES

Researchers have examined whether there are gender differences in children's understanding of display rules, concepts of lying, and use of cues to infer deception. They have found gender differences in children's understanding of display rules during middle childhood, with girls displaying greater understanding or endorsement of display rules than boys (Carlson, Moses, & Hix, 1998; Underwood, Coie, & Herbsman, 1992). Also, during middle childhood, girls have been found to be more likely to regulate their emotional expression in response to a disappointing gift than are boys (Davis, 1995). A number of studies found no gender differences in children's concepts of lying (e.g., Bussey, 1992; Stouthamer-Loeber, 1991). Gender differences have been found in research that were most directly related to the present study. Rotenberg (1991) found that, in sixth grade, boys more frequently reported that a range of cues (including gaze and limb movement) revealed deception than did girls. Gender differences were not found in fourth- and second-grade children. Because of the conflicting and complex pattern of findings, predictions about gender differences were not advanced in the present study.

OVERVIEW OF THE STUDY
AND HYPOTHESES

The present study was designed to investigate children's use of cues associated with anxiety to infer deception. The children were asked to judge peers who systematically displayed variations in gaze and limb movements accompanying their verbal communications. The study was designed to reveal children' s cue use by assessing (a) their responses to concrete stimuli, (b) the effects of variations in cues on inferred deception, and (c) the specific direction of the association between the variation in cues and inferred deception (e.g., that greater lying is attributed to indirect gaze than to direct gaze). On the basis of Rotenberg's (1991) findings, it was expected that children's use of cues associated with anxiety would increase linearly across middle childhood. Because use of limb movement cues and use of gaze cues were assumed to reflect the children's inference of a common underlying principle, anxiety, we expected that there would be a correlation between the children's use of the two cues. In that vein, it was necessary to carry out pilot studies to determine whether adults and children believed that anxiety is associated with indirect rather than direct gaze and with active limb movements rather than nonactive limb movements.

METHOD

Participants

The participants were 24 children (12 boys, 12 girls) from each of kindergarten, second, fourth, and sixth grades in two public elementary schools. The schools were located in low to middle socioeconomic residential districts in Thunder Bay, Ontario, Canada. The mean ages of the children in the four grades were 5 years 11 months, 7 years 9 months, 10 years, and 12 years 5 months, respectively. The children's participation was secured by parental consent.

Construction of the Stimuli

The stimulus children shown in the videotapes were two girls and two boys who were in second through fourth grades and who attended acting schools in the region. Each stimulus child was videotaped while providing 12 verbal communications that were composed of liking (positive) and disliking (negative) statements regarding three objects (i.e., a movie, a television program, or a shirt). The stimulus children varied gaze, limb movements, and vocal pitch while making the statements. We varied gaze by having the stimulus child look to the side away from the camera (indirect gaze) and by having the child gaze directly at the camera (direct gaze). The stimulus children displayed normal (nonactive) limb movement while providing these communications. We varied limb movement by having the stimulus child rub his or her hands (active limb movement) and by keeping them still (nonactive limb movement). The stimulus children looked directly at the camera while providing these communications. Finally, the stimulus children were required to vary their pitch but, because they had considerable difficulty in that task, further consideration of those cues was not viable. (1) Because of technical difficulties, two sets of communications were not used.

Pilot Study 1. Undergraduate students (4 male, 4 female) enrolled in introductory psychology classes assisted in appraising the videotaped communications. The students were presented with the 10 sets of six communications and were required to judge how anxious the stimulus child providing the communication was. Judgments were made on a 5-point scale ranging from 1 (not at all anxious) to 5 (very anxious). The 2 × 10 (Anxiety Level of Cue: low vs. high × Set) one-way analysis of variance (ANOVA) on judgments of the limb movement cues with repeated measures on both variables yielded a main effect of anxiety level of cue only, $F(1, 7) = 20.26$, $p < .01$. As expected, the college students attributed greater anxiety to the stimulus children when they displayed active (high) rather than nonactive limb movements (low; Ms = 3.80 and 2.09, respectively; SDs not available for Ms). The comparable 2 × 10 ANOVA on judgments of the gaze cues yielded a main effect of anxiety level of cue only, $F(1, 7) = 5.52$, $p = .05$. Again, as expected, college students attributed greater anxiety to the stimulus children when they displayed indirect gaze (high) than direct gaze (low; Ms = 2.95 and 2.05, respectively).

Pilot Study 2. Children appraised the videotaped communications as well. The cues were presented to 10 kindergarten children (5 boys, 5 girls), 10 second-grade children (5 boys, 5 girls), and 10 fourth-grade children (6 girls, 4 boys). They were solicited from the same school as those tested in the primary study. The children were tested individually and were presented one of two randomly selected sets of cues comprising six communications. The children were required to explain what nervous meant and then judged on 4-point scales how nervous each stimulus child providing the communication was. Children at all grade levels were able to provide basic definitions of being nervous (e.g., "kinda like being scared"). The judgments of the gaze and limb movement cues were each subjected to 3 × 2 × 2 (Grade: kindergarten, second, and fourth × Gender: male vs. female × Anxiety Level of Cue: low vs. high) ANOVA with repeated measures on the latter variable. The ANOVA yielded main effects of anxiety level of cue for gaze cues, $F(1, 24) = 9.71$, $p < .010$, and for limb movement cues, $F(1, 24) = 12.93$, $p < .001$. Children attributed greater anxiety to the stimulus children when they displayed active (high) rather than nonactive limb movement cues (low; Ms = 3.20 and 2.13, respectively) and indirect gaze (high) rather than direct gaze cues (low; Ms = 2.80 and 2.00, respectively). The effects were not qualified by grade ($F < 1$), and the pattern was evident at each grade level.

Stimuli. The sets of communications that were used in the study were composed in the following fashion. The core communication in each set was composed of three negative statements and three positive statements. One block of 12 sets of those six communications was constructed so that it systematically varied by (a) the order in which the communications were presented, (b) the peers providing the communications, (c) the object of the communication (i.e., a movie, a television program, and a shirt), and (d) the three cues (including vocal pitch). The block of 12 sets of the six communications was replicated such that there was one in which the children were girls and another in which the children were boys. Each participant in the study received 1 set of six communications. The 12 sets of communications were assigned to the 12 participants in each cell of 2 × 4 (Gender × Grade) design such that there were equal frequencies for each cell of the positive and negative statements, the different stimulus children, the three objects of the statements, and three types of cues (including vocal pitch).

PROCEDURE

The participants were tested individually by the experimenter. Each participant was shown a videotape of the same-gender peers (stimulus children) presenting the six verbal communications. To ensure that the participant attended to the communications, we preceded each communication with a tone. After each communication was presented, the participant was asked to repeat what the peer had said (which all participants did with little error), and then the participant was asked to judge how much he or she thought the peer on the videotape was telling the truth. The participant was asked whether he or she (a) thought that the boy or girl was telling the truth (scored as 1), (b) was unsure whether the boy or girl was telling the truth or lying (scored as 2), or (c) thought that the boy or girl was lying (scored as 3).

RESULTS

The participants' lying judgments were scored such that larger numbers corresponded to greater lying (referred to as attributions of lying). The attributions of lying were subjected to 2 × 4 × 2 × 2 (Gender: male vs. female × Grade: kindergarten, second, fourth, and sixth × Type of Anxiety Cue: limb movement and gaze × Anxiety Level of Cue: high vs. low) ANOVAs with repeated measures on the last two variables. The ANOVA included separate tests of linear effects of grade and curvilinear (quadratic effects) of grade.

The ANOVA yielded a main quadratic effect of grade, $F(1, 93) = 16.19$, $p < .001$; both kindergarten and sixth-grade participants attributed more lying to the peers (Ms = 2.10 and 2.18, respectively) than did second- and fourth-grade participants (Ms = 1.91 and 1.80, respectively; ps < .050). The ANOVA also yielded a main effect of anxiety level of cue, $F(1, 93) = 9.17$, $p < .010$, that was qualified by a linear Grade × Anxiety Level of Cue interaction at a trend level, $F(1, 93)$ 2.88, $p < .100$. The means for this interaction are shown in Table 1. A priori t comparisons indicated that greater lying was attributed to high rather than low anxiety cues in fourth grade ($p < .050$, one-tailed) and sixth grade ($p < .010$, one-tailed). The comparisons for kindergarten and second grades did not yield significance.

Table 1. Mean Attributions of Lying as a Function of Anxiety Level of the Cue and Grade

	Grade			
Anxiety Level of Cue	Kindergarten	Second	Fourth	Sixth
High	2.23	1.92	1.95	2.54
Low	1.96	1.90	1.65	1.81

Note. Higher numbers denote greater attributions of lying.

Because the overall analysis may have obscured the extent to which the participants used each type of anxiety cue, separate 2 × 2 (Gender × Anxiety Level of Cue) ANOVAs were carried out on the attributions of lying for each type of cue. The ANOVA on the limb movement cues yielded a main effect of anxiety level of cue, $F(1, 93) = 4.80$, $p < .05$; the participants attributed more lying to peers when they showed active (high) rather than nonactive (low) limb movement (Ms = 2.13 and 1.81, respectively). This ANOVA yielded a quadratic effect of grade, $F(1, 93) = 7.57$, $p < .01$, that was similar to the one yielded by the ANOVA on both types of cues.

The ANOVA on the gaze cues yielded a main effect of anxiety level of cue, $F(1, 93) = 6.08$, $p < .01$; participants attributed more lying to the peers when they showed indirect (high) rather than direct gaze (low; Ms = 2.19 and 1.84, respectively). Again, the ANOVA yielded a quadratic effect of grade, $F(1, 93) = 8.72$, $p < .01$, replicating the pattern yielded by the ANOVA on both types of cues.

Relation Between the Use of Limb Movement and Gaze Cues

Difference scores were calculated as an index of the extent to which participants used each of the two types of cues. Specifically, the difference was calculated between (a) the lying attributed to active and the lying attributed to nonactive limb movements and (b) the lying attributed to indirect gaze and the lying attributed to direct gaze. Consistent with expectation, there was a significant correlation between the two difference scores, $r(96) = .21$, $p < .05$.

DISCUSSION

The pilot studies supported the conclusion that adults and children associated indirect rather than with direct gaze and active rather than nonactive limb movements with anxiety. When considered in the context of other research on beliefs about deception (Kraut, 1978; Riggio & Friedman, 1983; Vrij

& Semin, 1996), the present findings support the conclusion that indirect gaze and limb movements represent prevalent beliefs about the behavioral indices of anxiety in Western culture. It should be highlighted that the second pilot study also indicated that the stimulus cues depicted in the videotapes were identifiable even for kindergarten children.

The findings of the primary study support the conclusion that children use indirect gaze and active limb movements to infer deception. The children attributed more lying to the peers who displayed indirect gaze rather than direct gaze and who displayed active rather than nonactive limb movement. This result is consistent with Rotenberg's (1991) observations that children frequently identified gaze and limb movements as cues for deception. As in Rotenberg's study, linear effects of age were found. Fourth- and sixth-grade children showed greater evidence of use of those cues than did kindergarten and second-grade children. No gender differences or interaction between gender and age were found in the children's use of the anxiety cues to infer deception.

Some caution should be taken in concluding that young children (kindergartners and second graders) are not able to use cues associated with anxiety to infer deception. Young children may be able to infer deception from (a) other types of cues associated with anxiety or (b) combinations of the gaze and limb movement cues. With respect to the latter suggestion, close inspection of the findings reveals that kindergarten children showed some tendency to attribute greater lying to indirect rather than direct gaze and active rather than nonactive limb movements. Consequently, young children may be able to use a combination of those anxiety cues to infer deception (e.g., indirect gaze and active limb movement concurrently).

A quadratic age pattern was found in children's attributions of lying in which both kindergarten and sixth-grade children attributed more lying to the peers on the videotapes than did second- and fourth-grade children. Given the lack of theory and research bearing on such age relations, further research replicating that pattern is required before conclusions can be advanced with confidence.

Researchers need to address why children used gaze and limb movements that are associated with anxiety to infer deception and why age differences in such cue use were observed. There was one finding yielded by the study that was suggestive. Consistent with our expectations, children's use of each of two types of cues, as assessed by differences scores, were correlated. This expectation was based on the notion that children's use of limb movement cues and use of gaze cues to infer deception reflect their inference of a common underlying principle, specifically anxiety. As previously discussed, various lines of theories are potentially relevant to the observed patterns: theory of mind, children's concepts of lying, understanding of display rules, and learned physiological cues for anxiety. The latter was not regarded as viable, however, because children and adults do not display greater indirect gaze and limb movements when deceiving. The observed age differences in cue usage are consistent with two lines of re search in particular: children's understanding of display rules and children's concepts of lying. Researchers have documented increases in both domains across middle childhood (Bussey, 1992; Gnepp & Hess, 1986). It is possible that children learn the anxiety cue display rule by direct socialization practices (Saarni & Salisch, 1993) in which parents verbally convey that rule to their children.

There are several directions for future research. First, researchers should continue to examine children's use of other cues associated with anxiety, such as vocal pitch, to infer deception. Second, the method used in the present study was designed to examine children's use of cues associated with anxiety to infer deception with minimal reliance on children's linguistic and cognitive representational ability (i.e., responses to concrete stimuli depicting variations in the target cues). Researchers should examine whether children will articulate the anxiety display rule, with the recognition, however, that children's articulation of that rule depends on their linguistic and cognitive representational ability. Third, researchers should examine concurrent and developmental links between children's use of the cues associated with anxiety (e.g., indirect gaze and active limb movements) to infer deception and their performance on tasks used to assess theory of mind, understanding of display rules, and the concept of lying. The results may shed light on some of the cognitive underpinnings of children's use of such cues to infer deception. Fourth, in an attempt to assess parental antecedents, researchers should examine the potential link between parents' use of cues and their children's use of cues associated with anxiety to infer deception.

Thanks are extended to John Bonofiglio for his assistance with the research. Portions of this article were presented at the Society for Research on Child Development Biennial Meeting in Minneapolis, MN, April 2001.

Address correspondence to Ken J. Rotenberg, Department of Psychology Keele University, Staffordshire ST5 5BG, UK; k.j.rotenberg@keele.ac.uk (e-mail).

NOTE

(1) The children were required to vary their pitch (high vs. low) during their verbal communications. Unfortunately, the children showed considerable difficulty in doing that task. Most attempts to display normal pitch appeared to be forced, and most attempts to display high pitch were manifested in a varying pitch during the course of the communication. This result is consistent with research demonstrating that children display limited ability to control their vocal cues in order to deceive others (Feldman & Custrini, 1991; Feldman, Jenkins, & Popoola, 1979; also see DePaulo, 1992). The variations in vocal pitch were carried out independently of the variations of the other two types of cues (limb movement and gaze) and, therefore, could be treated separately.

CRITICAL THINKING QUESTIONS

1. Theory of mind in children is an ability that shows drastic improvement at around 4 years of age, and links to cognitive development suggest that it is in part a maturational process. Discuss how the maturation of this system impacts the understanding of lying.
2. Rotenberg and Sullivan cite research that shows that girls appear to have a greater understanding of emotional display rules than boys do, and that they are better at regulating their emotional expression to display a feeling that they are not feeling (e.g., pleasure at receiving a disappointing gift). Given these findings, who would you suspect would be a better liar: boys or girls? Why?
3. In the Rotenberg and Sullivan study, the researchers pretested the notion that adults and children use indirect gaze and active limb movements as a cue to anxiety. Why was it important to determine if this was a correct assumption prior to studying the link between these physical indices and judgments of lying? How would a negative result have impacted their main study?

REFERENCES

Bugental, D. E., Kaswan, J. W., & Love, L. R. (1970). Perception of contradictory meanings conveyed by verbal and nonverbal channels. *Journal of Personality and Social Psychology, 16,* 647–655.

Buller, D. B., & Aune, R. K. (1987). Nonverbal cues to deception among intimates, friends, and strangers. *Journal of Nonverbal Behavior; 11,* 269–290.

Bussey, K. (1992). Lying and truthfulness: Children's definitions, standards, and evaluative reactions. *Child Development, 63,* 129–137.

Carlson, S. M., Moses, L. J., & Hix, H. R. (1998). The role of inhibitory processes in children's difficulties with deception and false belief. *Child Development, 69,* 672–691.

Carpendale, J. I., & Chandler, M. J. (1996). On the distinction between false belief understanding and subscribing to an interpretive theory of mind. *Child Development, 67,* 1686–1706.

Chandler, M., Fritz, A. S., & Hala, S. (1989), Small-scale deceit: Deception as a marker of two-, three-, and four-year-olds' theories of mind. *Child Development, 60,* 1263–1277.

Davis, T. L. (1995). Gender differences in masking negative emotions: Ability or motivation? *Developmental Psychology, 31,* 660–667.

Davis, T. L. (2001). Children's understanding of false beliefs in different domains: Affective vs. physical. *British Journal of Developmental Psychology, 19,* 47–58.

DePaulo, B. M. (1992). Nonverbal behavior and self-presentation. *Psychological Bulletin, 111,* 203–243.

DePaulo, B. M., Jordan, A., Irvine, A., & Laser, P. S. (1982). Age changes in the detection of deception. *Child Development, 53,* 701–709.

DePaulo, B. M., Stone, J. I., & Lassiter, G. D. (1985). Deceiving and detecting deceit. In B. R. Schlenker (Ed.), *The self and social life* (pp. 323–370). New York: McGraw Hill.

Feldman, R. S., & Custrini, R. J. (1991). Learning to lie: Children's nonverbal communication of deception. In J. S. Lockard & D. L. Paulhus (Eds.), *Self-deception* (pp. 41–53). Englewood Cliffs, NJ: Prentice Hall.

Feldman, R. S., Jenkins, L., & Popoola, O. (1979). Detection of deception in adults and children via facial expressions. *Child Development, 50,* 350–355.

Flavell, J. H. (2000). Development of children's knowledge about the mental world. *International Journal of Behavioral Development, 24,* 15–23.

Friedman, H. S. (1979). The interactive effects of facial expressions of emotion and verbal messages on perceptions of affective meaning. *Journal of Experimental Social Psychology, 15,* 453–469.

Gardner, D., Harris, P. L., Ohmoto, M., & Hamazaki, T. (1988). Japanese children's understanding of the distinction between real and apparent emotion. *International Journal of Behavioral Development, 11,* 203–218.

Gnepp, J., & Hess, D. L. R. (1986). Children's understanding of verbal and facial display rules. *Developmental Psychology, 22,* 103–108.

Goedert, H. W., Rill, H. G., & Gerhard, V. (2001). Psychophysiological differentiation of deception: The effects of electrodermal lability and mode of responding on skin conductance and heart rate. *International Journal of Psychophysiology, 40,* 61–75.

Harris, P. L., Donnelly, K., Guz, G. R., & Pitt-Watson, R. (1986). Children's understanding of the distinction between real and apparent emotion. *Child Development, 57,* 895–909.

Jones, D. C., Abbey, B. B., & Cumberland, A. (1998). The development of display rule knowledge: Linkages with family expressiveness and social competence. *Child Development, 69,* 1209–1222.

Joshi, M. S., & MacLean, M. (1994). Indian and English children's understanding of the distinction between real and apparent emotion. *Child Development, 65,* 1372–1384.

Kraut, R. (1978). Verbal and nonverbal cues in the perception of lying. *Journal of Personality and Social Psychology, 36,* 380–391.

Lewis, M. (1993). The development of deception. In M. Lewis & C. Saarni (Eds.), *Lying and deception in everyday life* (pp. 90–105). New York: Guilford Press.

Lewis, M., Stanger, C., & Sullivan, M. W. (1989). Deception in 3-year-olds. *Developmental Psychology, 25,* 439–443.

Peterson, C. C., Peterson, J., & Seeto, D. (1983). Developmental changes in ideas about lying. *Child Development, 54,* 1529–1535.

Piaget, J. (1965). *The moral judgment of the child.* Harmondsworth, UK: Penguin Books.

Riggio, R. E., & Friedman, H. 5. (1983). Individual differences and cues to deception. *Journal of Personality and Social Psychology 45,* 899–915.

Rotenberg, K. J. (1991). Children's cue use and strategies for detecting deception. In K. J. Rotenberg (Ed.), *Children's interpersonal trust: Sensitivity to lying, deception and promise violations* (pp. 43–57). New York: Spring-Verlag.

Rotenberg, K. J., Simourd, L., & Moore, D. (1989). Children's use of verbal-nonverbal consistency principle to infer truth and lying. *Child Development, 60,* 309–322.

Ruffman, T., Olson, D. R., Ash, T., & Keenan, T. (1993). The ABCs of deception: Do young children understand deception in the same way as adults? *Developmental Psychology, 29,* 74–87.

Saarni, C. (1979). Children's understanding of display rules of expressive behavior. *Developmental Psychology, 15,* 424–429.

Saarni, C., & Salisch, M. (1993). The socialization of emotional dissemblance. In M. Lewis & C. Saarni (Eds.), *Lying and deception in everyday life* (pp. 106–125). New York: Guilford Press.

Stouthamer-Loeber, M. (1991). Young children's verbal misrepresentations of reality. In K. J. Rotenberg (Ed.), *Children's interpersonal trust: Sensitivity to lying, deception and promise violations* (pp. 20–42). New York: Springer-Verlag.

Underwood, M. K., Coie, J. D., & Herbsman, C. R. (1992). Display rules for anger and aggression. *Child Development, 63,* 366–380.

Vrij, A., Edward, K., & Bull, R. (2001). Stereotypical verbal and nonverbal responses while deceiving others. *Personality and Social Psychology Bulletin, 27,* 899–909.

Vrij, A., & Semin, G. R. (1996). Lie experts' beliefs about nonverbal indicators of deception. *Journal of Nonverbal Behavior, 20,* 65–80.

Wimmer, H., Gruber, S., & Peruer, J. (1984). Young children's conception of lying: Lexical realism-moral subjectivism. *Journal of Experimental Child Psychology, 37,* 1–30.

Zuckerman, M., DePaulo, B. M., & Rosenthal, R. (1981). Verbal and nonverbal communication of deception. In L. Berkowitz (Ed.), *Advances in experimental and social psychology* (Vol. 14, pp. 1–59). New York: Academic Press.

Zuckerman, M., Koestner, R., & Driver, R. (1981). Beliefs about the cues associated with deception. *Journal of Nonverbal Behavior, 6,* 105–114.

14

Attachment and Social Relationships

The Ties That Bond: Adult Romantic and Sexual Styles May Grow Out of Parent-Child Affiliations

Bruce Bower

Psychological research suggests that childhood relationships with caregivers form three possible orientations toward attachment in children and adults: secure, ambivalent, and avoidant. Evolutionary explanations for attachment behavior are discussed.

More than 50 years ago, as World War II's horrors and hatreds raged, British psychoanalyst John Bowlby bucked the global tide, delving into what he suspected were the roots of love. Bowlby took seriously Sigmund Freud's notion that individuals unconsciously orchestrate adult relationships on the basis of feelings and reactions originally evoked by childhood caretakers. He felt that the Viennese psychiatrist's idea had an untapped potential for exploring grown-up intimacies.

Bowlby, now deceased, first noted extensive delinquency in boys who had seen little of their mothers as infants. He also came across reports of a "failure to thrive" in youngsters reared in institutions and cared for by rotating squads of nurses.

Soon afterwards, Bowlby came to appreciate caregiver–child attachments, as he called them, in many animals whose young require extensive care. For instance, ducklings instinctively trail after any larger creature who regularly offers them aid and comfort, whether it's a mother duck or a curious scientist. On the darker side, monkeys who grow up clinging to the cold, unresponsive body of a wire-mesh substitute mother become social misfits, cowering and staring blankly out of hollow eyes.

Bowlby theorized that the human species has made a heavy evolutionary investment in mutual bonds. An innate attachment system, consisting of behaviors and physiological responses that weave pairs of individuals into interdependent units, increases both the survival of helpless infants and the reproductive success of their parents.

On the basis of childhood ties to core adult protectors, he proposed, kids develop implicit expectations about how people operate in relationships. These working models of intimacy, which are presumably open to revision as one's social world expands, provide a blueprint for adult romantic pairings.

His conception of attachment as an evolutionary product that organizes interpersonal life from cradle to grave sparked little interest among developmental researchers. Instead, they applied Bowlby's ideas solely to the study of mother-child interactions. In the last decade, however, a growing number of scientists has embraced attachment theory as a useful perspective from which to explore the evolution of close relationships among adults.

"There seems to be little room for doubt that the same mechanism that evolved to tie infants to their caregivers was exploited by natural selection for keeping adult partners together," write psychologists Debra Zeifman and Cindy Hazan, both of Cornell University, in a chapter of *Evolutionary Social Psychology* (1997, Mahwah, N.J.: Lawrence Erlbaum).

The evolutionary reasons for plugging the infant-caregiver attachment system into an adults-only mating game are subject to dispute. Some researchers suspect that a lifelong capacity for social intimacy evolved as a single type of interpersonal glue, binding infants to their caregivers and tying sexual partners to one another so they can provide consistent care to offspring. Others regard caregiver-infant bonds as comprising a spectrum of arrangements that can steer a child's mating proclivities down any number of paths, from heartfelt monogamy to conniving promiscuity.

Much research has documented the existence of three possible attachment orientations in children and adults: secure, ambivalent, and avoidant.

Most infants achieve secure attachment to at least one caregiver. For these youngsters, the mother or another adult consistently responds to their needs, serves as a source of comfort at times of distress, and offers a safe base from which to explore the world. Adults with a secure orientation tend to have trusting, lasting relationships in which they share intimate information and work out conflicts through compromise.

Ambivalent youngsters receive inconsistent support that sows doubts about the caregiver's availability. Desperate attempts by these kids to attract adult attention are combined with an angry resistance to being soothed. Ambivalent adults view themselves poorly and become preoccupied with keeping their romantic partners close at hand and firmly committed to the relationship.

Avoidant infants get repeatedly rejected by their caregivers; and steer clear of them when upset. Novel surroundings evoke tentative or compulsive behavior but no attempts to seek adult support. Avoidant adults either look down upon or dread any hints of emotional intimacy.

Although some people seem poorly suited to marriage, enduring relationships between pairs of adults represent "the norm for our species," according to Zeifman and Hazan. For millennia, the most successful parents have been those who stayed together and made sure that their children learned skills for survival, finding a mate, and raising offspring, the psychologists theorize.

Their argument contrasts with a prior proposal that adults are, by nature, "serial monogamists" who experience infatuations only long enough to raise a child for about 4 years (SN: 11/27/93, p. 362).

Clear majorities of both sexes report a desire for lasting sexual relationships that appears to stem from the attachment system, Zeifman and Hazan argue. In cross-cultural surveys, men and women alike report that the most crucial qualities of a potential mate are kindliness, empathy, and intelligence.

Such qualities also nurture secure attachment in infants, who carefully monitor a caregiver's kindness and perceptiveness, as well as his or her familiarity.

For adults, the many divorces that occur in the first few years of marriage may reflect the failure of spouses to form a psychological attachment, Zeifman and Hazan theorize. When attachment does flower, its effects transcend each person's contribution to the relationship, and partners may get more than they bargained for—true love.

Unlike other social relationships, full-blown attachments contain four defining features, according to Zeifman and Hazan. In such duos, partners maintain close physical proximity and seek each other out at times of danger or stress. In addition, the relationship is conceived of as a secure base in the world, and separation sparks emotional distress or, in the case of one partner's death, grief.

In a survey of young and middle-aged adults, Zeifman and Hazan found that attachments meeting all of these criteria had been formed almost exclusively with parents and sexual partners. In a comparable study of teenagers, such attachments to peers were rare overall but appeared fairly often in the minority who had ambivalent or avoidant orientations toward their parents.

Such results contribute to evidence that adult attachment evolved to keep sexual partners together, contend Lynn C. Miller and Stephanie A. Fishkin, both psychologists at the University of Southern California in Los Angeles. In groups of Stone Age hunters and foragers, they propose, adults who melded into stable relationships and gave their children plenty of support were more likely to experience enjoyable sex and raise their youngsters to maturity.

However, the rise of city life over the past 10,000 years has introduced more people to abject poverty and shrunk the number of supportive friends and family living near one another, Miller and Fishkin argue. Such conditions often breed parents who are unable or unwilling to stay together and who are unprepared to offer sensitive care to their kids, in their view.

A child's ambivalent or avoidant responses to such parents may gear him or her toward a secondary strategy of pursuing short-term relationships instead of a long-term attachment.

Preliminary data gathered by the USC scientists support their theory that long-term relationships are the natural state. In two studies that consisted of more than 600 male and female college students, most members of both sexes said that they preferred having either one or two sexual partners over the next 30 years rather than none or more than two. There was no overall difference among students reporting different forms of attachment to their parents.

Only men who had experienced cold, distant relationships to their fathers departed sharply from this pattern, most often citing a desire for four future partners.

Researchers known as evolutionary psychologists take a different approach to the study of adult attachment styles. Mating patterns arise from individual strategies to promulgate one's genes, either by producing and raising more offspring or by aiding the survival of other kin, these scientists contend. A range of sexual approaches emerges from an evolved repertoire of attachment styles, no single one of which is likely to have predominated in Stone Age life, they theorize.

For instance, David M. Buss of the University of Texas at Austin argues that differences in early childhood attachments prod individuals toward pursuing one of a variety of sexual strategies, which may include stable relationships for securely attached folks and casual sex for those with ambivalent orientations.

This work draws heavily on a model presented in 1991 by Jay Belsky, a psychologist at Pennsylvania State University in State College, and his colleagues. They theorized that times of relative safety and abundance produce warm parental care. Secure attachments set the stage for delayed sexual maturity, mating with one or a few people, and intensive nurturing of the children's own offspring, they say.

In contrast, parental care grows chillier in times marked by scarce food and shaky prospects for survival. Caregivers treat infants in harsh, dismissive ways.

Under such circumstances, youngsters develop ambivalent or avoidant attachments that imbue them with a sense of fatalistic opportunism regarding close relationships. Belsky proposes that these children often begin puberty early, mate with many people, and devote limited effort to raising the resulting brood—characteristics that he considers advantageous in hard times.

Ambivalent attachment may also have evolved as a means of inducing enough helpless dependency in some children—perhaps in those with an introverted disposition—that they become adult "helpers at the nest" for parents or other kin, Belsky speculates.

"Secure and insecure [attachment] patterns evolved as responses to care-giving practices that enable individuals to successfully reproduce, or at least once did so in [certain] environments," Belsky writes in the upcoming *Handbook of Attachment Theory and Research* (J. Cassidy and P. Shaver, eds., New York: Guilford). Stone Age ecological conditions may have promoted attachment patterns that don't appear in modern cultures, he suggests.

Full-blown attachment, with its various interactions, may in fact occur only in childhood, adds psychologist Lee A. Kirkpatrick of the College of William and Mary in Williamsburg, Va. Long-term sexual relationships depend only on the ability to experience the emotion of love, Kirkpatrick contends.

It will take a decade or more to evaluate fully the competing evolutionary explanations of attachment, remarks psychologist Jeffry A. Simpson of Texas A&M University in College Station. In the meantime, he says, attachment theory looks like a promising tool for studying close adult ties in the here-and-now.

Consider an as-yet-unpublished study by Simpson of the ways in which college students with different attachment styles handle a visceral threat to a dating relationship. Each member of dating duos that had been together for an average of 16 months first completed a battery of surveys on their attitudes toward relationships and love, from which attachment scores were generated. They were then videotaped as they evaluated and discussed slides of highly attractive and moderately attractive students with their dating partner looking on. Afterwards, all the volunteers watched their videotapes and noted their thoughts and feelings at specific points.

While looking at photos of men, the secure women frequently checked to see if their partner were upset, threatened, or jealous, whereas avoidant women tended to ignore their partners. Men, regardless of attachment style, checked their partners most often during evaluations of the most attractive alternatives.

When viewing the videotapes, the secure men exhibited a greater willing-ness than other men to reveal their dismay as their partners rated potential dates.

When shown a videotape of their partner rating the photos, many participants—including those displaying secure attachment styles—exhibited little understanding of their partner's thoughts and feelings. Simpson attributes this tendency, first reported in a study that did not measure attachment (SN: 3/23/96, p. 190), to a need to keep knowledge about relationship-threatening thoughts at bay in order to preserve the romantic status quo.

Ambivalent women, however, showed keen empathic insight when their partners rated other women. At the same time, they felt much discomfort and insecurity about themselves and their relationships.

Constant worry about the commitment of partners may impel ambivalent women to try to monitor and control them at all times, Simpson says. That smothering strategy may backfire when the women make uncomfortable discoveries about their beaus that provoke jealousy and may derail relationships.

Four months after the study, break-ups were most likely to have occurred between pairs in which both partners have ambivalent attachment styles.

Scientists need to examine how attachment styles influence the responses of married partners to threatening situations, Simpson notes.

That's a challenge John Bowlby would have undoubtedly relished.

CRITICAL THINKING QUESTIONS

1. Zeifman and Hazan argue that the most successful parents would be those who stayed together and raised their children as a partnership. Furthermore, they imply that this type of romantic attachment system would have been the best reproductive strategy for parents irrespective of variations in ecological conditions (e.g., relative abundance of resources versus a relative scarcity of resources). Given that evolution typically acts to reduce variation in traits strongly selected for, why would the insecure attachment categories still exist in humans? Shouldn't natural selection have "weeded them out" over the course of human evolution?

2. Belsky, by contrast, argues that the ways in which parents treat children depend in part upon local ecological conditions. These caregiving variations lead to variations in children's attachment classifications, which then serve as cues for the formation of adult romantic attachment. For example, Belsky theorizes that secure children tend to develop romantic relationships in their adult years marked by close, enduring partnerships. By contrast, avoidant babies characteristically prefer short term, less intimate liaisons with others, and ambivalent babies tend to remain close to parents and kin at the expense of personal romantic relationships. Essentially, Belsky argues that caregiving during infancy is a cue to likely ecological conditions during adulthood. Why should ecological conditions during adulthood impact what type of adult romantic relationship would be most adaptive? Under what conditions would insecure romantic attachments result in greater fitness gains for parents than secure attachments?

15

The Family

Role of Genotype in the Cycle of Violence in Maltreated Children

Avshalom Caspi, Joseph McClay, Terrie E. Moffitt, Jonathan Mill, Judy Martin, Ian W. Craig, Alan Taylor, and Richie Poulton

We studied a large sample of male children from birth to adulthood to determine why some children who are maltreated grow up to develop antisocial behavior, whereas others do not. A functional polymorphism in the gene encoding the neurotransmitter-metabolizing enzyme monoamine oxidase A (MAOA) was found to moderate the effect of maltreatment. Maltreated children with a genotype conferring high levels of MAOA expression were less likely to develop antisocial problems. These findings may partly explain why not all victims of maltreatment grow up to victimize others, and they provide epidemiological evidence that genotypes can moderate children's sensitivity to environmental insults.

Childhood maltreatment is a universal risk factor for antisocial behavior. Boys who experience abuse—and, more generally, those exposed to erratic, coercive, and punitive parenting—are at risk of developing conduct disorder, antisocial personality symptoms, and of becoming violent offenders (1, 2). The earlier children experience maltreatment, the more likely they are to develop these problems (3). But there are large differences between children in their response to maltreatment. Although maltreatment increases the risk of later criminality by about 50%, most maltreated children do not become delinquents or adult criminals (4). The reason for this variability in response is largely unknown, but it may be that vulnerability to adversities is conditional, depending on genetic susceptibility factors (5, 6). In this study, individual differences at a functional polymorphism in the promoter of the monoamine oxidase A (MAOA) gene were used to characterize genetic susceptibility to maltreatment and to test whether the MAOA gene modifies the influence of maltreatment on children's development of antisocial behavior.

The MAOA gene is located on the X chromosome (Xp11.23-11.4) (7). It encodes the MAOA enzyme, which metabolizes neurotransmitters such as norepinephrine (NE), serotonin (5-HT), and dopamine (DA), rendering them inactive (8). Genetic deficiencies in MAOA activity have been linked with aggression in mice and humans (9). Increased aggression and increased levels of brain NE, 5-HT, and DA were observed in a transgenic mouse line in which the gene encoding MAOA was deleted (10), and aggression was normalized by restoring MAOA expression (11). In humans, a null allele at the MAOA locus was linked with male antisocial behavior in a Dutch kindred (12). Because MAOA is an X-linked gene, affected males with a single copy produced no MAOA enzyme—effectively, a human knockout. However, this mutation is extremely rare. Evidence for an association between MAOA and aggressive behavior in the human general population remains inconclusive (13–16).

Circumstantial evidence suggests the hypothesis that childhood maltreatment predisposes most strongly to adult violence among children whose MAOA is insufficient to constrain maltreatment-induced changes to neurotransmitter systems. Animal studies document that maltreatment stress (e.g., maternal deprivation, peer rearing) in early life alters NE, 5-HT, and DA neurotransmitter systems in ways that can persist into adulthood and can influence aggressive behaviors (17–21). In humans, altered NE and 5-HT activity is linked to aggressive behavior (22). Maltreatment has lasting neurochemical correlates in human children (23, 24), and although no study has ascertained whether MAOA plays a role, it exerts an effect on all aforementioned neurotransmitter systems. Deficient MAOA activity may dispose the organism toward neural hyperreactivity to threat (25). As evidence, phenelzine injections, which inhibit the action of monoamine oxidase, prevented rats from habituating to chronic stress (26). Low MAOA activity may be particularly problematic early in life, because there is insufficient MAOB (a homolog of MAOA with broad specificity to neurotransmitter amines) to compensate for an MAOA deficiency (8).

Based on the hypothesis that MAOA genotype can moderate the influence of childhood maltreatment on neural systems implicated in antisocial behavior, we tested whether antisocial behavior would be predicted by an interaction between a gene (MAOA) and an environment (maltreatment).

A well-characterized variable number tandem repeat (VNTR) polymorphism exists at the promoter of the MAOA gene, which is known to affect expression. We genotyped this polymorphism in members of the Dunedin Multidisciplinary Health and Development Study, a sample without population stratification confounds (27). This birth cohort of 1,037 children (52% male) has been assessed at ages 3, 5, 7, 9, 11, 13, 15, 18, and 21 and was virtually intact (96%) at age 26 years.

The study offers three advantages for testing gene-environment (G x E) interactions. First, in contrast to studies of adjudicated or clinical samples, this study of a representative general population sample avoids potential distortions in association between variables (28, 29). Second, the sample has well-characterized environmental adversity histories. Between the ages of 3 and 11 years, 8% of the study children experienced "severe" maltreatment, 28% experienced "probable" maltreatment, and 64% experienced no maltreatment (27). (Maltreatment groups did not differ on MAOA activity, χ^2 (2) = 0.38, $P = 0.82$, suggesting that genotype did not influence exposure to maltreatment.) Third, the study has ascertained antisocial outcomes rigorously. Antisocial behavior is a complicated phenotype, and each method and data source used to measure it (e.g., clinical diagnoses, personality checklists, official conviction records) is characterized by different strengths and limitations. Using information from independent sources appropriate to different stages of development, we examined four outcome measures (27). Adolescent conduct disorder was assessed according to criteria of the *Diagnostic and Statistical Manual of Mental Disorders* (DSM-IV); convictions for violent crimes were identified via the Australian and New Zealand police; a personality disposition toward violence was measured as part of a psychological assessment at age 26; symptoms of antisocial personality disorder were ascertained at age 26 by collecting information about the study members from people they nominated as "someone who knows you well." A common-factor model fit the four measures of antisocial behavior well (27), with factor loadings ranging from 0.64 to 0.74, showing that all four measures index liability to antisocial behavior.

Using moderated regression analysis, we predicted scores on a composite antisocial index comprising the four measures of antisocial behavior (27) (Fig. 1) [Figure Omitted]. (All figures referenced can be found within the online version of this article, at http://www.infotrac-college.com.)

The main effect of MAOA activity on the composite index of antisocial behavior was not significant (b = 0.01, $SE = 0.09$, $t = 0.13$, $P = 0.89$), whereas the main effect of maltreatment was significant (b = 0.35, $SE = 0.07$, $t = 4.82$, $P < 0.001$). A test of the interaction between MAOA activity and maltreatment revealed a significant G x E interaction (b = −0.36, $SE = 0.14$, $t = 2.53$, $P = 0.01$). This interaction within each genotype group showed that the effect of childhood maltreatment on antisocial behavior was significantly weaker among males with high MAOA activity (b = 0.24, $SE = 0.11$, $t = 2.15$, $P = 0.03$) than among males with low MAOA activity (b = 0.68, $SE = 0.12$, $t = 5.54$, $P < 0.001$).

We conducted further analyses to test if the G x E interaction was robust across each of the four measures of antisocial behavior that made up the composite index. For all four antisocial outcomes, the pattern of findings was consistent with the hypothesis that the association between maltreatment and antisocial behavior is conditional, depending on the child's MAOA genotype (G x E interaction P = 0.06, 0.05, 0.10, and 0.04, respectively). For adolescent conduct disorder (Fig. 2A) [Figure Omitted], maltreated males (including probable and severe cases) with the low-MAOA activity genotype were more likely than nonmaltreated males with this genotype to develop conduct disorder by a significant odds ratio (OR) of 2.8 [95% confidence interval (CI): 1.42 to 5.74]. In contrast, among males with high MAOA activity, maltreatment did not confer significant risk for conduct disorder (OR = 1.54, 95% CI: 0.89 to 2.68). For adult violent conviction (Fig. 2B) [Figure Omitted], maltreated males with the low-MAOA activity genotype were more likely than nonmaltreated males with this genotype to be convicted of a violent crime by a significant odds ratio of 9.8 (95% CI: 3.10 to 31.15). In contrast, among males with high MAOA activity, maltreatment did not confer significant risk for violent conviction (OR = 1.63, 95% CI = 0.72 to 3.68). For self-reported disposition toward violence (Fig. 2C) [Figure Omitted] and informant-reports of antisocial personality disorder symptoms (Fig. 2D) [Figure Omitted], males with the low-MAOA activity genotype who were maltreated in childhood had significantly elevated antisocial scores relative to their low-MAOA counterparts who were not maltreated. In contrast, males with high MAOA activity did not have elevated antisocial scores, even when they had experienced childhood maltreatment.

These findings provide initial evidence that a functional polymorphism in the MAOA gene moderates the impact of early childhood maltreatment on the development of antisocial behavior in males. Replications of this G x E interaction are now needed. Replication studies should use valid and reliable ascertainments of maltreatment history and should obtain multiple measures of antisocial outcomes, in large samples of males and females (30). If replicated, the findings have implications for research and clinical practice. With regard to research in psychiatric genetics, knowledge about environmental context might help gene-hunters refine their phenotypes. Genetic effects in the population may be diluted across all individuals in a given sample, if the effect is apparent only among individuals exposed to specific environmental risks. With regard to research on child health, knowledge about specific genetic risks may help to clarify risk processes. Numerous biological and psychological processes have been put forward to explain why and how experiences of maltreatment are converted into antisocial behavior toward others (17, 24, 31–34), but there is no conclusive evidence that any of these processes can account for the progression from childhood maltreatment to later criminal violence. Moreover, some youngsters make the progression, but others do not, and researchers have sought to understand why (35). The search has focused on social experiences that may protect some children, overlooking a potential protective role of genes. Genes are assumed to create vulnerability to disease, but from an evolutionary perspective they are equally likely to protect against environmental insult (36). Maltreatment studies may benefit from ascertaining genotypes associated with sensitivity to stress, and the known functional properties of MAOA may point toward hypotheses, based on neurotransmitter system development, about how stressful experiences are converted into antisocial behavior toward others in some, but not all, victims of maltreatment.

Until this study's findings are replicated, speculation about clinical implications is premature. Nonetheless, although individuals having the combination of low-activity MAOA genotype and maltreatment were only 12% of the male birth cohort, they accounted for 44% of the cohort's violent convictions, yielding an attributable risk fraction (11%) comparable to that of the major risk factors associated with cardiovascular disease (37). Moreover, 85% of cohort males having a low-activity MAOA genotype who were severely maltreated developed some form of antisocial behavior. Both attributable risk and predictive sensitivity indicate that these findings could inform the development of future pharmacological treatments.

Avshalom Caspi, (1,2) Joseph McClay, (1) Terrie E. Moffitt, *(1,2), Jonathan Mill, (1) Judy Martin, (3) Ian W. Craig, (1) Alan Taylor, (1) Richie Poulton (3)

(1) Medical Research Council Social Genetic, and Developmental Psychiatry Research Centre, Institute of Psychiatry, King's College, London SE5 8AF, UK. (2) Department of Psychology, University of Wisconsin, Madison, WI 53706, USA. (3) Dunedin School of Medicine, Box 913, University of Otago, New Zealand.

*To whom correspondence should be addressed. E-mail: t.moffitt@iop.kcl.ac.uk

CRITICAL THINKING QUESTIONS

1. Caspi et al. state that children who were maltreated and children who were not maltreated did not differ on MAOA activity. If Caspi et al. had found the converse (i.e., that children who were maltreated more often had high levels of MAOA), what would this suggest about the influence of their genotype on maltreatment?

2. MAOA is a sex-linked gene. In other words, the gene coding for MAOA expression is found on the X-chromosome. Explain how this impacted the researchers' choice to limit their analysis to males in their sample.

REFERENCES AND NOTES

1. C. S. Widom, *Science* 244, 160 (1989).

2. M. Rutter, H. Giller, A. Hagell, *Antisocial Behavior by Young People* (Cambridge Univ. Press, Cambridge, 1998).

3. M. K. Keiley, T. R. Howe, K. A. Dodge, J. E. Bates, G. S. Pettit, *Dev. Psychopathol. 13,* 891 (2001).

4. C. S. Widom, in *Handbook of Antisocial Behavior,* D. M. Stoff, J. Breiling, J. D. Maser, Eds. (Wiley, New York, 1997).

5. K. S. Kendler, *Arch. Gen. Psychiatry 58,* 1005 (2001).

6. M. Rutter, J. Silberg, *Annu. Rev. Psychol. 53,* 463 (2002).

7. E. R. Levy et al., *Genomics 5,* 368 (1989).

8. J. C. Shih, K. Chen, M. J. Ridd. *Annu. Rev. Neurosci. 22,* 197 (1999).

9. D. C. Rowe, *Biology and Crime* (Roxbury, Los Angeles, 2001).

10. O. Cases et al., *Science 268,* 1763 (1995).

11. J. C. Shih, R. F. Thompson, *Am. J. Hum. Genet. 65,* 593 (1999).

12. H. G. Brunner, M. Nelen, X. O. Breakefield, H. H. Ropers, B. A. van Oost, *Science 262,* 578 (1993).

13. A. F. Jorm et al., *Psychiatr. Genet. 10,* 87 (2000).

14. A. Parsian, C. R. Cloninger, *Psychiatr. Genet. 11,* 89 (2001).

15. S. B. Manuck, J. D. Flory, R. E. Ferrell, J. J. Mann, M. F. Muldoon, *Psychiatry Res. 95,* 9 (2000).

16. J. Samochowiec et al., *Psychiatry Res. 86,* 72 (1999).

17. J. D. Bremner, E. Vermetten, *Dev. Psychopathol. 13,* 473 (2001).

18. D. D. Francis, M. J. Meany, Curr. Opin. Neurobiol. 9, 128 (1999).

19. G. W. Kraemer, M. H. Ebert, D. E. Schmidt, W. T. McKinney, *Neuropsychopharmacology 2,* 175 (1989).

20. A. J. Bennett et al., *Mol. Psychiatry 7,* 188 (2002).

21. S. J. Suomi, in *Handbook of Developmental Psychopathology,* A. J. Sameroff, M. Lewis, S. Miller, Eds. (Plenum, New York, in press).

22. M. E. Berman, R. J. Kavoussi, E. F. Coccaro, in *Handbook of Antisocial Behavior,* D. M. Stoff, J. Breiling, J. D. Maser, Eds. (Wiley, New York, 1997).

23. D. Pine et al., *Arch. Gen. Psychiatry. 54,* 839 (1997).

24. M. De Bellis, *Dev. Psychopathol. 13,* 539 (2001).

25. V. Morell, *Science 260,* 1722 (1993).

26. H. E. Ward et al., *Pharmacol. Biochem. Behav. 60,* 209 (1998).

27. Materials and methods are available as supporting material on Science Online.

28. P. Cohen, J. Cohen, *Arch. Gen. Psychiatry 41,* 1178 (1984).

29. A. F. Jorm, S. Easteal, *Soc. Psychiatry Psychiatr. Epidemiol. 35,* 1 (2000).

30. This study focused on males because their single X chromosome yields two straightforwardly characterized MAOA genotypes: high activity (63% in this sample) and low activity (37%). Females, having two copies of the X chromosome, fall into two homozygous groups, high–high (42%

in this sample), low–low (12%), and a third heterozygous group, low–high (46%), that cannot be characterized with certainty because it is not possible to determine which of the two alleles is inactivated for each female participant. Given the rarity in females of both the low–low genotype (12%) and severe antisocial outcomes, such as violent conviction (2%), our cohort of 481 females, 11% of whom were severely maltreated, was too small to support all of the analyses reported here for males. However, adolescent conduct disorder could be analyzed, revealing that girls with the low–MAOA activity genotype were more likely to develop conduct disorder by a significant odds ratio of 5.5 (95% CI: 1.0 to 32.0) if they were maltreated. In contrast, among girls with high MAOA activity, maltreatment did not confer significant risk for conduct disorder (OR = 1.7, 95% CI: 0.75 to 4.2). This suggests that high MAOA activity exerts a protective influence against maltreatment for girls as well as boys, and raises the possibility that further research into X-linked genotypes may help to explain one of the least understood facts about serious antisocial behavior: the sex difference (38).

31. K. A. Dodge, J. E. Bates, G. S. Pettit, *Science 250* 1678 (1990).

32. S. D. Pollak, D. Cicchetti, R. Klorman, J. T. Brumaghim, *Child Dev. 68*, 773 (1997).

33. D. Glaser, *J. Child Psychol. Psychiatry 41*, 97 (2000).

34. D. Cicchetti, F. A. Rogosch, *Dev. Psychopathol. 13*, 783 (2001).

35. S. S. Luthar, D. Cicchetti, B. Becker, *Child Dev. 71*, 543 (2000).

36. A. V. S. Hill, *Br. Med. Bull. 55*, 401 (1999).

37. S. M. Grundy, R. Paternak, P. Greenland, S. Smith, V. Fuster, *J. Am. Coll. Cardiol. 34*, 1348 (1999).

38. T. E. Moffitt, A. Caspi, M. Rutter, P. A. Silva, *Sex Differences in Antisocial Behavior: Conduct Disorder, Delinquency, and Violence in the Dunedin Longitudinal Study* (Cambridge Univ. Press, Cambridge, 2001).

39. We thank P. Silva, founder of the Dunedin Multidisciplinary Health and Development Study, Air New Zealand, and the study members, their families, and friends. Supported by the Health Research Council of New Zealand, the University of Wisconsin Graduate School, and by grants from the U.K. Medical Research Council and the U.S. National Institute of Mental Health (MH49414, MH45070). The study protocol was approved by the institutional review boards of the participating universities.

SUPPORTING ONLINE MATERIAL

www.sciencemag.org/cgi/content/full/297/5582/851/DC1

Materials and Methods

Tables S1 and S2

16

Developmental Psychopathology

Prevalence of Alzheimer's Disease and Vascular Dementia: Association with Education: the Rotterdam Study

Alewijn Ott, Monique M.B. Breteler, Frans van Harskamp, Jules J. Claus, Tischa J.M. van der Cammen, Diederick E. Grobbee, and Albert Hofman

Elderly people with higher levels of education may be at a lower risk of developing dementia than those with lower levels of education. Dementia is a mental disorder characterized by personality changes, confusion, disorientation and impairment of memory and judgment. Researchers studied 7528 patients aged 55 to 106 years to determine the frequency of dementia and its relation to education. Of the 7528 patients, 474 (6.3%) were diagnosed with dementia. Alzheimer's disease, a disorder causing confusion, memory loss, disorientation and restlessness, accounted for 72% (339) of the dementia cases. As the patient's level of education increased, the risk of

Prevalence of Alzheimer's disease and vascular dementia: association with education. The Rotterdam study. Alewijn Ott; Monique M.B. Breteler; Frans van Harskamp; Jules J. Claus; Tischa J.M. ver der Cammen; Diederick E. Grobbee; Albert Hofman from British Medical Journal, April 15, 1995 v.310 n6985 p970(4). Copyright 1995 British Medical Association.

dementia decreased. People with only primary education or low level vocational training were significantly more likely to develop dementia than those with medium-level vocational training or university-level education. The rate of dementia also rose with age, ranging from less than 1% among patients aged 55 to 59 years to about 43% among patients aged 95 years and older.

ABSTRACT

Objective—To estimate the prevalence of dementia and its subtypes in the general population and examine the relation of the disease to education.

Design—Population based cross sectional study.

Setting—Ommoord, a suburb of Rotterdam.

Subjects—7528 participants of the Rotterdam study aged 55–106 years.

Results—474 cases of dementia were detected, giving an overall prevalence of 6.3%. Prevalence ranged from 0.4% (5/1181 subjects) at age 55–59 years to 43.2% (19/44) at 95 years and over. Alzheimer's disease was the main subdiagnosis (339 cases; 72%); it was also the main cause of the pronounced increase in dementia with age. The relative proportion of vascular dementia (76 cases; 16%), Parkinson's disease dementia (30; 6%), and other dementias (24; 5%) decreased with age. A substantially higher prevalence of dementia was found in subjects with a low level of education. The association with education was not due to confounding by cardiovascular disease.

Conclusions—The prevalence of dementia increases exponentially with age. About one third of the population aged 85 and over has dementia. Three quarters of all dementia is due to Alzheimer's disease. In this study an inverse dose-response relation was found between education and dementia—in particular, Alzheimer's disease.

INTRODUCTION

In many populations the proportion of elderly people is growing steadily. Owing to shifts in the population pyramid and increased life expectancy the number of people aged 75 and over in the Netherlands has increased by 65% in the past 20 years.[1] Similar increases have occurred in other countries and will have a major impact on future health care Costs.[2] Dementing disorders are common in elderly and, especially, very old people.[3] Studies of their prevalence rates and determinants are of medical and social importance.

We studied the prevalence of dementia and its subtypes among 7528 subjects in the population-based Rotterdam study with special reference to its association with level of education.

POPULATION AND METHODS

The Rotterdam study is a prospective population-based study of several important groups of diseases of old age[4,5]—namely, neurological, cardiovascular, locomotor, and ophthalmological. Between 1990 and 1993 all participants were subjected to detailed interview examination in order to collect baseline data and ascertain their health status. In a sub-study the prevalence of dementia was assessed by a three phase approach. Firstly, all participants were screened with a brief cognitive test. Screen positive subjects then underwent additional testing, and those whose results suggested a possibility of dementia were either subjected to detailed examination or had their medical records used to confirm the diagnosis and establish the type of dementia.

Study Population

All residents of the Rotterdam suburb of Ommoord aged 55 and over (including those living in institutions) were invited to participate in the Rotterdam study. Of the 10275 eligible subjects, 7983 (78%) accepted. Of the eligible subjects, 7528 (73%) were screened for cognition in the dementia study, the remaining subjects being lost through death or refusal.

Measurements

The brief cognitive test for dementia comprised a combined mini-mental state examination[6] and geriatric mental state schedule (GMS-A, organic level).[7] The test was administered by trained research assistants. Screen positive subjects had a mini-mental state examination score of 25 or less or a geriatric mental state score of 1 or more. Screen positive subjects were subsequently examined by a physician with the CAMDEX (Cambridge examination for mental disorders of the elderly) diagnostic interview,[8] which included an interview with an informant. Participants who scored less than 80 on the CAMDEX cognitive test or who had higher scores but were suspected of dementia clinically were asked to participate in a third, extensive examination. In this diagnostic phase they were examined by a neurologist, had a brain scan (by magnetic resonance imaging), and were tested by a neuropsychologist.

Of the screen positive subjects, 92% underwent the CAMDEX diagnostic interview. Many subjects with dementia were resident in six homes for elderly people, which were included in the study. These homes had psychogeriatric departments. Often the subjects were already known to be demented. In these subjects and the 8% of screen positive subjects who refused the CAMDEX diagnostic interview or could not be examined diagnostic information was obtained from the general practitioner, physicians in the homes, neurologists, or the Rotterdam Regional Institute for Ambulatory Mental Health Care.

During the initial interview the attained level of education was assessed according to the standard classification of education,[9] comparable to the international standard classification of education (Unesco, Paris, 1976). In the standard classification of education seven levels are recognised. In our analysis we combined the four highest levels into one category, thus obtaining four levels: (1) primary education (which applied to 26% of participants); (2) low level vocational training (20%); (3) medium level secondary education (15%); (4) medium level vocational training to university level (39%).

Three indicators of cardiovascular disease (stroke, myocardial infarction, and peripheral atherosclerotic disease), as detailed elsewhere,[10] were examined as possible confounders in the relation between education and dementia. A history of stroke was determined by interview or informant interview in dementia patients. Confirmation of the stroke by a treating physician was required. A previous myocardial infarction was assessed from an electrocardiogram. Suspected abnormalities according to preset criteria were all reviewed by a cardiologist. The presence of peripheral atherosclerotic disease was assumed if the ankle-arm index (ratio between tibial and brachial systolic blood pressure, measured supine) was <0.9 on one side.

Diagnosis of Dementia

Dementia was diagnosed according to the American Psychiatric Association's criteria (DSM-III-R).[11] The subdiagnosis of Alzheimer's disease was based on criteria produced by the National Institute of Neurological and Communicative Disorders and Stroke and the Alzheimer's Disease and Related Disorders Association.[12] Both possible and probable cases of Alzheimer's disease were grouped in this category. For the subdiagnosis of vascular dementia the DSM-III-R definition of multi-infarct dementia was used.

The dementia type at the onset of the disease was ascertained. Some patients with Alzheimer's disease develop symptoms of vascular dementia in the course of the disease, usually after a stroke, which may result in a sudden worsening of dementia.[13] We classified these patients as Alzheimer type with cerebrovascular disease. Parkinson's disease dementia was diagnosed when the dementia started after the onset of idiopathic parkinsonism. The three most important other dementias were alcoholrelated dementia, tumourrelated dementia, and dementia associated with normal pressure hydrocephalus. In five patients insufficient information was available to make a subdiagnosis.

On the basis of the clinical dementia rating scale[14] and the minmental state examination score a division was made between severe impairment (clinical dementia rating scale over 2 or minmental state examination score under 16, referred to below as severe dementia) and mild to moderate impairment. In the overall prevalence figures all dementia cases, from mild to severe, were included.

Data Analysis

The prevalence of dementia and its subtypes was calculated as the percentage of dementia by sex and five year age groups. Multivariate logistic regression was used to analyse the association between educational status and dementia.

The odds ratio as estimated from the logistic model was used as our measure of association and referred to as relative risk. With dementia or one of the subtypes of dementia as outcome variable we compared the levels of education adjusted for age (numerical variable) and sex. The highest educational level (category 4) was used as reference. The trend in the relative risk for dementia by education was tested with level of education as a linear trend variable in the logistic regression analysis.

By adding stroke, myocardial infarction, or peripheral atherosclerotic disease as covariates in the logistic regression model we checked if these cardiovascular indicators caused substantial changes in the relative risks associated with the various levels of education.

RESULTS

Table I shows the numbers of participants in the dementia study together with their age distribution and the proportion resident in institutions. Of the 7528 study participants, 474 (6.3%) were demented—3.8% (112/2939) of men, 7.9% (362/4589) of women. (All tables and figures referenced can be found within the online version of this article, at http://www.infotrac-college.com.) Age and sex specific prevalences of dementia are shown in table II and figure 1[Figure Omitted]. With the exception of the age category 80–89 years there were no major differences in prevalence between men and women. At ages 80–89 years women had a higher prevalence of dementia than men. About one third of all demented people had severe dementia; this applied to both men and women.

Prevalences of Alzheimer's disease, vascular dementia, Parkinson's disease dementia, and other dementias are shown in figure 2 [Figure Omitted]. Overall, 72% of the dementias were of Alzheimer type, 16% were vascular dementia, 6% were Parkinson's disease dementia, and 5% were other dementias. Table III shows the sex specific prevalences and numbers of cases of the types of dementia in 10 year age groups. There were no substantial differences between men and women in the proportions of dementia types.

The relative risks of dementia (adjusted for age and sex) decreased with increasing educational status (fig 3) [Figure Omitted]. Among people with the two lowest levels of education significantly more dementia was diagnosed than among those with the highest level of education (relative risks 3.2 (95% confidence interval 2.2 to 4.6) and 2.0 (1.3 to 3.2) respectively). Similarly for Alzheimer's disease the two lowest educational levels were associated with increased relative risks (4.0 (2.5 to 6.2) and 2.3 (1.3 to 4.1) respectively). For vascular dementia, only the least educated were at significantly increased risk (2.1 (1.0 to 4.5)). Other dementias, including Parkinson's disease dementia, were not significantly associated with education. The trend of a higher prevalence of dementia with less education was highly significant

($P < 0.0001$). Similar trends were observed for Alzheimer's disease and vascular dementia ($P < 0.0001$ and $P = 0.01$, respectively).

Adding one or a combination of the indicators of cardiovascular disease did not decrease the inverse relation between educational status and dementia, suggesting that the presence of cardiovascular disease did not explain the association between dementia and education.

Discussion

We have presented detailed age specific prevalences of dementia and dementia subtypes that indicate Alzheimer's disease as the main contribution to the exponential increase of dementia with age. Our data also show a consistent trend of a higher risk of dementia with lower educational level. This effect of educational status could not be explained by a confounding effect of cardiovascular disease.

All recent population based studies on the prevalence of dementia with standardised diagnostic criteria show an exponential increase with age and a predominance of Alzheimer's disease as the cause of the dementia. However, age specific prevalences vary considerably between studies. This may be due to study design, population sampling methods, or real geographical variations.

Our study is the largest European study of its kind, allowing more precise estimates of prevalence. Compared with a pooled reanalysis of 12 European studies,[3] our study showed slightly lower prevalences below the age of 75 and slightly higher prevalences above age 80. Differences in screening and the type of population were the most likely causes. A high sensitivity and specificity of the diagnostic procedure was ensured by the three phase comprehensive diagnostic work up.[15]

A major concern in prevalence studies is nonparticipation. The Rotterdam study, of which the dementia study was only a part, had a fairly high participation rate (almost 80%). However, the non-response may have been selective. If non-response distorted the study results it probably produced an underestimate of the prevalence of dementia. We consider it unlikely that non-response influenced the proportions of dementia.

Without confirmation at necropsy, subtyping dementia remains uncertain. Also the current diagnostic criteria that we used are of limited accuracy, which complicates all large population based dementia studies and which we could not improve even by basing the subdiagnoses on a great number of reliable data. Alzheimer's disease was the main contributor to the steep increase in dementia prevalence with age. We observed only a little increase with age in vascular dementia and even less in Parkinson's disease dementia and other dementias. We classified primary Alzheimer's disease complicated by cerebrovascular disease and Alzheimer's disease. This may be why we found a somewhat higher prevalence of Alzheimer's disease than reported in other European studies.[16]

In common with other studies, we found a higher prevalence of dementia in groups with less education.[17–21] It has been suggested that the education effect could be due to diagnostic bias. There is, indeed, a possibility that early dementia might be missed in a highly educated person, though we do not think that this occurred often in our series because the combined mini–mental state examination and geriatric mental state schedule is a very sensitive screening test.[15] That the education effect also applied to vascular dementia led us to consider whether the association of education with dementia might be due to confounding by cardiovascular disease. This is possible, as cardiovascular disease is associated with both education and dementia. Particularly vascular dementia—but also Alzheimer's disease—is correlated with cardiovascular disease[13, 22, 23] and cardiovascular disease is more prevalent in people with less education.[24, 25] However, control for possible confounding by cardiovascular disease did not substantially decrease the magnitude of the association of education with dementia, nor with the subtypes of dementia.

In conclusion, this large population based study suggests that the prevalence of Alzheimer's disease increases with age and that dementia—particularly Alzheimer's disease—is inversely related to educational status.

We are grateful to staff of the Rotterdam study centre for help in data collection, Caroline van Rossum for providing the encoded educational levels, and Inge de Koning for neurophysiological testing. We also acknowledge the collaboration with the general practitioners in Ommoord and the RIAGG (Rotterdam Regional Institute for Ambulatory Mental Health Care) Noord Rotterdam. This study was made possible by financial support from the NESTOR stimulation programme for geriatric research in the Netherlands (Ministry of Health and Ministry of Education), the Netherlands Organisation for Scientific Reseach (NWO), the Netherlands Praeventionfund, and the municipality of Rotterdam.

CRITICAL THINKING QUESTIONS

1. Ott et al. found an inverse relationship between the prevalence of Alzheimer's disease and level of education attained in participants such that those people with higher levels of education were at a lower risk for developing the disease. While one might assume that this means education confers a protective buffer against the development of Alzheimer's, can you think of any other variables that might be related both to the development and diagnosis of Alzheimer's as well as to difficulties in attaining higher levels of education? Is there an alternative to the analysis the authors propose?

2. If, by contrast, education does indeed provide a buffer to dementia, what does this imply about the plasticity of the mind later in life? What about higher levels of education might protect people from dementia?

3. Given that roughly 6 percent of study participants were classified as demented, what is the researcher's obligation regarding informed consent?

If a prospective research participant is incapable of understanding what participation entails, is it ethical to pursue that line of inquiry nonetheless? What safeguards ought to be in place for studies such as this one?

KEY MESSAGES

- In a case finding study in a general population 9% of subjects aged 65 and over and 34% of subjects aged 85 and over had dementia
- Of all cases of dementia, 72% were cases of Alzheimer's disease
- The pronounced increase in prevalence of dementia with age was due to a substantial increase in Alzheimer's disease
- Alzheimer's disease was more often diagnosed in less educated people
- The association between dementia and education could not be explained by cardiovascular disease comorbidity

REFERENCES

[1] Netherlands Central Bureau of Statistic. Statistisch jaarboeck. The Hague: 's-gravenhage, 1974, 1994.

[2] Schneider EL, Guralnik JM. The aging of America. Impact on health care costs. *Jama* 1990;263:2335–40.

[3] Hofman A, Rocca WA, Brayne C, Breteler MMB, Clarke M, Coop B, et al. The prevalence of dementia in Europe: a collaborative study of 1980–1990 findings. *Int J Epidemiol* 1991;20:735–48.

[4] Hofman A, Grbbee DE, de Jong PTVM, van den Ouweland FA. Determinants of disease and disability in the elderly. The Rotterdam elderly study. *Eur J Epidemiol* 1991;7:403–22.

[5] Breteler MMB, den Ouweland FA, Grobbee DE, Hofman A. A8 community-based study of dementia: the Rotterdam elderly study. *Neuroepidemiology* 1992;11(suppl 1):23–8.

[6] Folstein MF, Folstein SE, McHugh PR. "Mini-mental state." A practical method for grading the cognitive state of patients for the clinician. *J Psychiatr Res* 1975;12:189–98.

[7] Copeland JRM, Keleher MJ, Kellet JM, Courlay AJ, Gurland BJ, Fleiss JL, et al. A semi-structured clinical interview for the assessment of diagnosis and mental state in the elderly. The geriatric mental state schedule. I. Development and reliability. *Psychol Med* 1976;6:439–49.

[8] Roth M, Huppert FA, Tym E, Mountjoy CQ. *CAMDEX, the Cambridge examination for mental disorders of the elderly.* Cambridge: Cambridge University Press, 1988.

[9] Netherlands Central Bureau of Statistics. *Standard classification of education SOI-1978*. Voorburg: Netherlands Central Bureau of Statistics, 1987.

[10] Breteler MMB, Claus JJ, Grobbee DE, Hofman A. Cardiovascular disease and the distribution of cognitive function in elderly people: the Rotterdam study. *BMJ* 1994;308:1604–8.

[11] American Psychiatric Association. *Diagnostic and statistical manual of disorders,* 3rd edition, revised. Washington, DC: American Psychiatric Association, 1987.

[12] McKhan G, Drachman D, Folstein M, Katzman R, Price D, Stadlan EM. Clinical diagnosis of Alzheimer's disease: report of the NINCDS-ADRDA Work Group under the auspices of Department of Health and Human Services Task Force on Alzheimer's Disease. *Neurology* 1984;34:939–44.

[13] Roman GC, Tatemichi TK, Erkinjuntti T, Cummings JL, Masdeu JC, Garcia JH, et al. Vascular dementia: diagnostic criteria for research studies, Rep., of the NINDS-AIREN international workshop. *Neurology* 1993;43:250–60.

[14] Hughes CP, Berg L, Danziger WL, Coben LA, Martin RL. A new clinical scale for the staging of dementia. *Br J Psychiatry* 1982;140:566–72.

[15] Dewey ME, Copeland JRM, Hofman A, eds. *Case finding finding for dementia in epidemiological studies. Eurodem report 1*. Liverpool: Institute of Human Aging, 1990.

[16] Rocca WA, Hofman A, Brayne C, Breteler MMB, Clarke A, Copeland JRM, et al. Frequency and distribution of Alzheimer's disease in Europe: a collaboration study of 1980–1990 prevalence findings. *Ann Neurol* 1991;30:381–90.

[17] Zhang M, Katzman R, Jin H, Cai G, Wang Z, Qu G, et al. The prevalence of dementia and Alzheimer's disease (AD) in Shanghai, China: impact of age, gender and education. *Ann Neurol* 1990;27:428–37.

[18] Rocca WA, Banaiuto S, Lippi A, Luciani P, Turtu F, Cavarzeran F, et al. Prevalence of clinically diagnosed Alzheimer's disease and other dementing disorders: a door-to-door survey in Appignano, Macerate Province, Italy. *Neurology* 1990;40:626–31.

[19] Dartigues JF, Gagnon M, Michel P, Letenneur L, Commenges D, Barberger-Gateau P, et al. Paquid, le programme de recherche Paquid sur l'epidemiologie de la demence methodes et resultats initiaux. *Rev Neurol* 1991;147:225–30.

[20] Katzman R. Education and the prevalence of dementia and Alzheimer's disease. *Neurology* 1993;43:13–20.

[21] Friedland RP. Epidemiology, education, and the ecology of Alzheimer's disease. *Neurology* 1993;43:246–9.

[22] Hashinski V. Multi-infarct dementia. *Neurol Clin* 1983;1:27–36.

[23] Poirier J, Davignon J, Bouthillier D, Kogan S, Bertrand P, Gauthier S. Apolipoprotein E polymorphism and Alzheimer's disease. *Lancet* 1993;342:697–9.

[24] Winkleby MA, Jatulis DE, Frank E, Fortmann SP. Socioeconomic status and health: now education, income, and occupation contribute to risk factors for cardiovascular disease. *Am J Public Health* 1992;82:816–20.

[25] Feldman JJ, Makuc DM, Kleinman JC, Cornoni-Huntley J. National trends in educational differentials in mortality. *Am J Epidemiol* 1989;129:919–33.

17

The Final Challenge: Death and Dying

How Long Is the Human Life-Span?

Marcia Barinaga

There are two competing theories regarding the human life-span. One holds that biological limits exist that begin to be felt around the age of 85. The other claims that there are no such limits. Some scientists in the first group think death due to old age arises from frailty of the body, observing that even minor insults to the body, such as the flu or a fall, often lead to death in older people. Others believe that diseases such as osteoporosis (a decrease in bone density) or atherosclerosis (accumulation of deposits in the blood vessels) are the prime causes of death in the elderly and that the development of these illnesses can be delayed or prevented, thereby extending the life-span. It is theorized by the latter group that if the major causes of death in the aging, such as heart disease, cancer and diabetes, were eliminated, people would tend to live well past the age of 85. While the records of people over the age of 85 in the United States are not accurate enough for such study, records in Sweden are extremely accurate and can be used to examine the life expectancy for people over 85. Studies have shown that the death rates in this age group have dropped dramatically in the last 50 years because more diseases can now be treated. A study with fruit flies, as an animal model for aging, shows that very old fruit flies do not grow biologically frail. Other studies in humans examined the idea of genetic determination of the age of death by using a

Reprinted (abstracted/excerpted) from "How long is the human life-span?" Marcia Barinaga. From Science, Nov. 15, 1991 v254 n5034 p936(3). Copyright 1991 AAAS.

registry of identical twins born between 1870 and 1890 and the age of death of the two twins if they died due to natural causes, at around the same age. Using a computerized model, the age of senescence was calculated to be around 110 years old, not 85. The expected length of the human life span will affect policies for care and treatment of the aging. The question arises whether money should be made available for the care and treatment of a population older than 85. (Consumer Summary produced by Reliance Medical Information, Inc.)

What is the biological limit to the human life-span? That question is, of course, riveting to all of us as we contemplate our own approaching mortality. But it also has some very practical medical and economic consequences—particularly in a "graying" society. Knowing how long our species is capable of living would influence strategies for combating the diseases of old age; it would also allow estimates of the future strain on social and medical programs expected to take care of the burgeoning number of older—and likely sicker—people.

But for the moment the question of whether there is a biological limit on the human life-span—and, if so, what that limit is—is very much a matter of debate. That debate may take a new turn next week when proponents of two distinctly different points of view come face to face over some new data at a session of the annual meeting of the Gerontological Society of America in San Francisco. One of the two, Stanford rheumotologist James Fries, is the leading current proponent of the notion of inborn limits; he thinks they kick in around age 85. Presenting the opposing viewpoint will be University of Minnesota demographer James Vaupel, who is currently a visiting professor at the Odense University Medical School in Denmark. Vaupel has been putting Fries' ideas to the test using Scandinavian population studies as well as data from fruit flies. His preliminary results, he says, show Fries to be wrong.

Fur may fly when Vaupel and Fries—who is widely known for his rhetorical skills—take the stage. "I can't predict what is going to happen when you get these two people up there, one saying [the limit to life] is 85, and the other saying there is no limit," says demographer Jay Olshansky of the University of Chicago, whose own work is in trying to estimate the practical limits to human life expectancy. But whether the symposium proceeds politely or not, it will surely provide a window onto a field that is now in a state of intellectual ferment.

Some of the parameters of the current debate were set 30 years ago when Leonard Hayflick, then of the Wistar Institute in Philadelphia, showed that cultured cells undergo a limited number of divisions. Hayflick extrapolated from this test-tube work to assert that the organs and tissues of the human body also run out of gas after some biologically predetermined time limit. This general notion, which Hayflick based on such findings as the fact that cells from older people undergo fewer doublings than those taken from younger people, became the central assumption in much of aging research.

Fries picked up what Hayflick began, with an article in 1980 in *The New England Journal of Medicine,* in which he argued that the human body is biologically destined to fall apart at about age 85, give or take a few years. "It is frailty, rather than disease," that kills people at very old ages, Fries told Science. "I think that by and large most people sort of sense this."

The concept of natural death is self-evident, says Fries, to anyone who has watched the gradual decline, or senescence, of older people, to the point where the tiniest insults—a fall that would have been trivial at age 20, a spell of hot weather, or a minor case of the flu—are enough to cause death. An elderly person may survive one insult only to succumb to another equally minor one. "I use the analogy of a sun-rotted curtain," adds Fries. "Try to sew up a tear in it and it just tears someplace else."

Fries supports his view with U.S. census statistics showing that the amount of expected life remaining for those who have reached age 65 has been constant in the United States for the past decade: 18.6 years, on average, for women and 14.7 years for men. He also plots U.S. life expectancy from birth and from age 65 for the past century and finds that the extrapolated lines converge at about age 85, suggesting, he says, that 85 is the biological limit to life. "I think that [85] is generally accepted," says Fries. "You can arrive at it in several different ways."

But Fries' conclusion isn't really as "generally accepted" as all that. Indeed, his view that most deaths of older people are due to biological senescence puts him at one end of a continuum that makes up today's debate on aging. Others take quite different views. For example, mathematical demographer Kenneth Manton of Duke University argues that many old people die from causes—such as osteoporosis or atherosclerosis—that were once considered the inevitable hallmarks of old age but that can now be prevented or delayed. Senescence, he says, is a catch-all term for those causes we don't yet understand or can't control. "If you approach and deal with a number of the major causes [of death]," says Manton, "you are incrementally dealing with what we had previously called senescence." Life expectancy, he argues, can and will continue to increase as medicine chips away at the diseases of old age.

As for the collection of U.S. statistics Fries uses to buttress his case, Manton argues that they are misleading: The plateau cited by Fries, Manton claims, was an artifact caused by changes in Medicare reimbursement policy introduced in the early 1980s that apparently decreased access to medical services for people over 85. Mortality rates for those over 65 have in fact resumed a downward trend in the last 3 years, he says. Moreover, both Manton and Chicago's Olshansky argue vehemently that Fries' intersecting lines make no sense. "The point at which those lines cross is influenced by things like infant mortality rates, which have nothing to do with the biological limits to life," Olshansky says.

Olshansky also laments that his own work has been misinterpreted as supporting Fries' conclusions, when in fact it does not. Olshansky and his colleagues showed that even if we were to eliminate most heart disease, cancer, and diabetes—the major causes of death in aging adults—life expectancy in the United States would not advance much beyond 85. But, says Olshansky, "we are talking about a practical limit, not a biological one." The point, he says, is not that you can't reduce death rates for 85-year-olds, but rather that even if you do, you won't change overall life expectancy figures, because there are too few people over 85 to influence the overall statistics.

Into this quagmire of arguments and counter-arguments steps Vaupel, who hopes to clarify matters with an infusion of new data. "In the past, this field has been characterized by debate," says Vaupel. "It's really time for science in this area to move beyond debate and start looking at evidence and models." Vaupel and his colleagues have been doing just that, and their findings, he says, are likely to produce, in his words, "a paradigm shift" away from the idea of biologically programmed death, at least at ages younger than 110 or so.

One problem with the present debate over life span, says Vaupel, is the poor quality of the data. Many of the arguments are based largely on U.S. figures. But Vaupel says these data for people over age 85 are notoriously flawed, citing studies by Gregory Spencer of the Census Bureau and Ansley Coale of Princeton showing that age exaggeration and misreporting make the numbers highly unreliable. Vaupel decided to turn instead to Swedish vital statistics—which have been kept with impeccable accuracy by the Lutheran church since 1750—to test Fries' claim that mortality rates at age 85 have barely changed since the turn of the century.

Vaupel and Swedish demographer and statistician Hans Lundstrom have been computerizing the records to look at trends in life expectancy for people 85 and older. What they have found, says Vaupel, is that the mortality rates for 85-year-old Swedes have dropped dramatically in the last 50 years. "Since World War II, death rates for 85-year-old Swedish females have been cut by more than one-third," says Vaupel; for men the progress has been half of that. Moreover, he says, the same is true for 90-, 95- and 100-year-olds as well.

Vaupel says his project is the first systematic examination of thousands of humans over age 85—a group called the "oldest old." But he didn't want to stop with humans. "The dispute [over the existence of a biological limit on life-span through senescent death] is not a dispute that holds only for humans, it's a dispute that holds for all different kinds of animals,' he says. "And virtually nothing is known about mortality rates at very old ages among any species except humans."

To remedy that, entomologist James Carey of the University of California, Davis, is collaborating with Vaupel and directing the construction of the largest life table ever made for any species, using 1 million Mediterranean fruit flies, at a mass rearing factory in Tapachula, Mexico. "The standard life table is [based on] 25 white mice," Carey says. "A few get into a few thousand individuals, but nothing approaches this." The medflies are reared in cages segregated by hatching date, and each day every dead fly from every cage is logged. It is necessary to use huge numbers of medflies, says Carey, to get a population of "oldest-old" that will allow meaningful analysis. Even if only 0.1% of the

1 million flies live to 100 days (roughly equivalent to 100 years for humans) that is still 1000 flies—a substantial number for analysis.

Carey expects to have recorded the death of the 1 millionth medfly by December, but the preliminary results are already in and they are surprising: The probability of dying increases for the first third of the flies' life-span and then appears to level off. "If you define senescence as the ever-increasing probability of dying," says Carey, "then the very oldest individuals are not senescing. It forces a complete re-think on the concept of senescence."

As if these two projects weren't enough, Vaupel and his colleagues have undertaken another pair of human-insect projects to address one of the underlying assumptions of the biological limit idea: the motion that senescence is determined, in Fries' words, by "the genetic characteristics of the species." That, says Vaupel, implies that individuals with identical sets of genes should begin to succumb to senescent death at roughly the same ages, provided they haven't succumbed to premature death.

To put that idea to the test, Vaupel turned again to Scandinavia, this time to life-span statistics compiled by the Danish twin registry on about 4000 twins born in Denmark between 1870 and 1890. He and Danish genetic epidemiologist Niels Holm are applying computer modeling to determine whether the pattern of death among the twins suggests a role for senescent death. The model that fits best, says Vaupel, is one in which all the deaths are "premature"—that is, due to accidents or disease—rather than senescent. "When we forced the computer to estimate the parameters for the senescent-death factor," he says, "it turned out that the level of senescent death was very close to zero. And the mean age at which senescent death occurred was not 85 but some number greater than 110."

To supplement the twin study, University of Minnesota entomologist James Curtsinger is looking at the life-spans of 16 different genetically identical strains of fruit flies. "They are analogous to twins," says Vaupel, "except that instead of having two Danes, you have 1000 drosophila." If those 1000 identical drosophila share genetically determined maximum life-spans, and the first 900 die prematurely," Vaupel says, "then you would expect the last 100 to die very close to each other." But Curtsinger has found that only one strain, under the most harsh rearing conditions tested, shows that pattern. Summarizing the findings of all four projects, Curtsinger says: "The [probability of dying] seems to be leveling off at the oldest ages. We are seeing it in all the projects."

Reactions to the preliminary findings of the Vaupel study range as broadly as one might expect in such a divided field. "I think there is going to be tremendous pay dirt there," says gerontologist Caleb Finch of the University of Southern California. Finch, who is the author of *Longevity, Senescence, and the Genome,* a book that deals with aging and senescence in a wide range of species, is particularly intrigued by Carey's medfly results. The steady increase of mortality with age has been shown for humans and suspected for other species, says Finch, but "Jim Carey's data look convincing that under some circumstances medflies don't show this." As to what the final word will be on biological limits to life, Finch declares it "a wait-and-see situation."

Olshansky is a bit skeptical, not of Vaupel's results but of their practical importance. "Vaupel, I believe, has incontrovertible evidence to indicate that if there is a 'death gene,' it certainly [doesn't exert its effects] before the age of 110 in humans." But, he says, while that may have disproved Fries' extreme position, it doesn't mean life expectancy will soar into the hundreds, as long as there are multiple, theoretically but not practically preventable diseases that are likely to kill people sooner.

Fries would not comment in detail until he sees the Vaupel data for himself next week. He says, however, that any findings Vaupel might have would not alter his conclusions, unless they were to change the slope of his intersecting life expectancy lines and shift the crossing point to a higher age. "If he had a curve that extrapolated to age 100, that would be counter evidence," he says, "but he doesn't; you know he doesn't. We have done it for the United States and Japan, and I know that the life expectancy data for age 85 aren't any better in Sweden." Fries adds that if Vaupel is seeing a decrease in mortality for 85-year-old Swedes, it must be due to reduction preventable deaths. "There are still preventable deaths at age 85," he says.

"If Fries is willing to admit that there is substantial premature death above age 85, that is something," Vaupel says. "That would mean we should be able to improve life expectancy." If this pre-symposium exchange is any indication, then the upcoming encounter may simply confirm what many in the field suspect: The debate over limits to life-span is far from over.

CRITICAL THINKING QUESTIONS

1. The Barinaga article presents two views of aging. Present the major arguments of each position. How strongly does the environment play a role in each of these approaches?

2. Typically, life expectancy is characterized as describing how long a person is expected to live. It is calculated by examining mortality rates of all individuals in a particular society. How might high rates of infant mortality bias this number? Should infant mortality rates impact life expectancy for those individuals who survive past the early years? Why or why not?

ADDITIONAL READING

J.F. Fries, "Aging, Natural Death and the Compression of Morbidity," *New England Journal of Medicine 303,* 130 (1980).

G.C. Myers and K.G. Manton, "Compression of Mortality: Myth or Reality?" *The Gerontologist 24,* 346 (1984).

J.F. Fries, "The Compression of Morbidity: Near or Far?" *The Milbank Quarterly 67*, 208 (1989).

S.J. Olshansky, B.A. Carnes, and C. Cassel, "In Search of Methuselah: Estimating the Upper Limits to Human Longevity," *Science 250*, 634 (1990).

InfoMarks: Make Your Mark

What Is an InfoMark?

It's a single-click return ticket to any page, any result, any search from InfoTrac College Edition.

An InfoMark is a stable URL, linked to InfoTrac College Edition articles that you have selected. InfoMarks can be used like any other URL, but they're better because they're stable—they don't change. Using an InfoMark is like performing the search again whenever you follow the link—whether the result is a single article or a list of articles.

How Do InfoMarks Work?

If you can "copy and paste," you can use InfoMarks.

When you see the InfoMark icon on a result page, its URL can be copied and pasted into your electronic document—Web page, word processing document, or email. Once InfoMarks are incorporated into a document, the results are persistent (the URLs will not change) and are dynamic.

Even though the saved search is used at different times by different users, an InfoMark always functions like a brand new search. Each time a saved search is executed, it accesses the latest updated information. That means subsequent InfoMark searches might yield additional or more up-to-date information than the original search with less time and effort.

Capabilities

InfoMarks are the perfect technology tool for creating:

- Virtual online readers
- Current awareness topic sites—links to periodical or newspaper sources
- Online/distance learning courses
- Bibliographies, reference lists
- Electronic journals and periodical directories
- Student assignments
- Hot topics

Advantages

- Select from over 15 million articles from more than 5,000 journals and periodicals
- Update article and search lists easily
- Articles are always full-text and include bibliographic information
- All articles can be viewed online, printed, or emailed
- Saves professors and students time
- Anyone with access to InfoTrac College Edition can use it
- No other online library database offers this functionality
- FREE!

How to Use InfoMarks

There are three ways to utilize InfoMarks—in HTML documents, Word documents, and email

HTML Document

1. Open a new document in your HTML editor (Netscape Composer or FrontPage Express).
2. Open a new browser window and conduct your search in InfoTrac College Edition.
3. Highlight the URL of the results page or article that you would like to InfoMark.
4. Right click the URL and click Copy. Now, switch back to your HTML document.
5. In your document, type in text that describes the InfoMarked item.
6. Highlight the text and click on Insert, then on Link in the upper bar menu.
7. Click in the link box, then press the "Ctrl" and "V" keys simultaneously and click OK. This will paste the URL in the box.
8. Save your document.

Word Document

1. Open a new Word document.
2. Open a new browser window and conduct your search in InfoTrac College Edition.
3. Check items you want to add to your Marked List.
4. Click on Mark List on the right menu bar.
5. Highlight the URL, right click on it, and click Copy. Now, switch back to your Word document.
6. In your document, type in text that describes the InfoMarked item.
7. Highlight the text. Go to the upper bar menu and click on Insert, then on Hyperlink.

8. Click in the hyperlink box, then press the "Ctrl" and "V" keys simultaneously and click OK. This will paste the URL in the box.
9. Save your document.

Email

1. Open a new email window.
2. Open a new browser window and conduct your search in InfoTrac College Edition.
3. Highlight the URL of the results page or article that you would like to InfoMark.
4. Right click the URL and click Copy. Now, switch back to your email window.
5. In the email window, press the "Ctrl" and "V" keys simultaneously. This will paste the URL into your email.
6. Send the email to the recipient. By clicking on the URL, he or she will be able to view the InfoMark.